Preface

S ixteen years ago my oldest daughter, Kelly, decided she wanted to be a ski racer. An eighty-mile round-trip commute separated our home in Anchorage from the race mountain, Alyeska, and the community of Girdwood. We commuted the first year, then rented and finally bought a small cabin next to a burbling creek, surrounded by towering hemlock trees.

Kelly's sister, Kara, had little choice but to ski and race, too, so most weekends found the entire family on the mountain, where the parents tended the racing gates and prayed that their daughters somehow survived their plunges down the mountain. The daughters went on to college and adulthood but we stayed. The little cabin burned down and my husband, Don, spent the next five years of weekends building a beautiful house for us while I became increasingly involved in Girdwood issues.

When Chris von Imhof, Alyeska's vice president and managing director, asked me to write a book on Girdwood and the resort, it gave me the excuse to meet dozens of fascinating people who so generously shared their lives and their photos with me.

Loverne Bercee provided the framework for this book with her collection of stories. Many details came from Don, who spent long hours in the library, and from photo editor Randy Brandon, who combed through thousands of photos for just the right mix. But it was the vision and support of Chris, who never gave up on Alyeska and its potential, that made this project possible.

The aurora borealis lights up the night sky above Mount Alyeska with its spectacular bands and curtains of light. October through March is the prime season for viewing the aurora, produced by charged particles from the sun striking natural gases in the earth's upper atmosphere. The Alyeska Prince Hotel offers a northern lights wake-up call as part of its service.

Introduction

Ernie's Mountain

Ernie Baumann wanted a ski mountain worthy of Alaska.

Like so many other post-World War II ski entrepreneurs, Baumann was a veteran of the elite 10th Mountain Division of high-elevation warriors, recruited from the ranks of the National Ski Patrol. He spent months in the early 1950s flying his Piper PA-14 around the hundreds of peaks that stretch from Seward to Mount McKinley, gradually narrowing his choice for a new ski area to an unnamed mountain on the east wall of Girdwood's Glacier Valley. The mountain fit his criteria perfectly: the right orientation, varied terrain, good snow—and ready access from Anchorage, less than forty miles away. Only a mile separated Baumann's mountain from a year-round gravel road.

Inspired by the name of Sun Valley, the nation's first destination ski resort, Baumann called the mountain Solar. With help from fellow skiers Sven Johanson and Joe Gayman, Baumann marshaled support from the handful of families who lived in Glacier Valley and the little town of Girdwood. The sell was easy. It was 1955 and Girdwood's economy was bust. A ski area could bring financial stability to the area.

Baumann filed the paperwork to purchase 160 acres of land at the base of the mountain under terms of a 1949 federal act that authorized the sale of public lands in Alaska. The parcel was sold at auction June 4, 1956—but it was Alyeska Ski Corp. that submitted the winning bid, not Baumann and his Mountain Sports Development Corp. Baumann had lost his financial backing, and he would lose his life just four years later when he crashed his plane in northwest Alaska on a trip to pick up polar bear hunters.

Alyeska Ski Corp. paid $3,325 for the land—money gathered by passing the hat among eleven Girdwood families who shared Baumann's vision. But the group thought the mountain that dominated their valley deserved an Alaska name, one as big and as bold as the peak itself.

Alaxsxag, suggested Chuck Nicolet, an Aleut who worked for the Alaska Railroad—"the great white land to the east," and one of the original names for Alaska. Aleut is a tough language to speak, much less spell, so the group simplified the word to Alyeska.

It was an appropriate name for this natural beauty that took millions of years and nature's most formidable forces to shape. The rock that forms the mountain came from thousands of miles away, slowly carried northward on the earth's giant crustal plates until it reached what is now Alaska, where intense pressure squeezed it upward. Then millions of tons of glacier ice took over, carving the mountain and grinding out the valley. Between at least four major episodes of ice advance and retreat, streams cut through the jumble of glacial debris, sculpting the valley and exposing the bedrock that eventually yielded gold.

Nestled on the surrounding mountainsides are the remnants of the last great glacial advance: Crow Glacier, Milk Glacier, Goat Glacier, Clear Glacier, Alyeska Glacier, Raven Glacier, and Eagle Glacier. Glacial melt, snowmelt, and rain feed the creeks that course through the valley, with the main stream aptly named Glacier Creek. Crow Creek joins Glacier Creek in the upper valley, followed by Winner Creek and then California Creek.

◄ ◄ ◄ **Ernie Baumann** [BAUMANN FAMILY]

◄ ◄ **Ernie Baumann demonstrates what he calls the artillery turn.** [BAUMANN FAMILY]

◄ **Powder hounds make fresh tracks off the center ridge on the upper slopes of Mount Alyeska. The mountain rises from the east wall of Glacier Valley, offering all the virtues of a great ski mountain: varying terrain, ample and consistent snowfall, and the proper orientation to ensure a long winter ski season.**

▲ **Two symmetrical snow peaks glow in the late afternoon light near the North Face area off the upper Glacier Bowl on Mount Alyeska.**

Members of the Anchorage Ski Club enjoy a summer outing in 1945 to Eagle Glacier, largest of the seven glaciers that ring Glacier Valley. Small aircraft regularly delivered skiers to the glacier in the 1950s and 1960s. [Anchorage Museum of History and Art]

Lining Glacier Valley is the community of Girdwood, an eclectic mixture of characters and curmudgeons, hovels and log palaces, surrounded by six million acres of mostly wilderness. It's a place where residents feel passionately about their future—and the postmistress knows most everyone's name.

Girdwood's roots date back more than a century, when the first miners arrived and needed a place to drink and eat and sleep. It's been a recreation center for the economic waves that followed: the railroaders, the road crews, and now those who seek adventure and relaxation in North America's northernmost rain forest.

The story of Girdwood and of the Alyeska Resort is one of unwavering optimism in a stunningly beautiful setting. It's a story best told through portraits of the natural surroundings and the people who made it so special. People like Axel Lindblad, who lost his fingers to frostbite and had a doctor cut a deep slit between his thumb and the stump of his index finger so he could hold a skinning knife. People like "Cap" Lathrop, Alaska's first homegrown millionaire, who chose Girdwood as the setting for the 1924 silent movie *The Chechahcos*.

Then there is Cynthia Toohey, who saved the historic Crow Creek Mine while raising her three children in a home with no running water, no electricity, no telephone. And Charlie Willis, the colorful president of Alaska Airlines, who helped persuade

Dwight Eisenhower to run for president and later chose what he called a whorehouse decor for Alyeska's Nugget Inn.

The ski slopes showcased their own memorable personalities: Don Conrad, who cleared trees with his chainsaw while blasting down the runs on skis; Doug Keil, who made it his crusade to help others with physical disabilities get the most out of life; Hilary Lindh and Tommy Moe, who honed their racing skills on this amazing mountain and went on to win Olympic silver and gold.

Alaska's Perfect Mountain is the story of Girdwood, Glacier Valley, and Mount Alyeska, but mostly it's the story of five extraordinary men whose vision and investment forever changed the little valley. They came from Europe and Asia, not America. Two had blue blood in their veins and one was once the richest man in the world:

- James Girdwood, an Irishman who rubbed shoulders with the likes of the wealthy Guggenheims and who gave his name to the community.
- François de Gunzburg, a French baron and member of the famous Rothschild banking family, who took a dream and turned it into a budding ski area with an international reputation.
- Chris von Imhof, scion of a German aristocratic family, who dedicated his life to creating a destination resort in Glacier Valley.
- Yoshiaki Tsutsumi, a man of long-term vision, who believes a promise made is a debt unpaid even when financial markets collapse.
- Per Bjorn-Roli, an exuberant Norwegian with the determination to develop Alyeska into a true international resort.

The story began with Ernie Baumann, a native of Germany, who set out to find the perfect Alaska ski mountain. He found it near a community that sprang up almost overnight when gold was found on Crow Creek. The little community, then called Glacier City, occupied a strategic spot that made it a natural stop on the Iditarod Trail and a construction camp during the building of the Alaska Railroad and later the Seward Highway.

When the highway opened in 1951, Baumann brought a handful of die-hard skiers to Girdwood and introduced them to local residents who wanted an economic anchor for their valley. A deal was struck and the journey began to turn Girdwood, Mount Alyeska, and Glacier Valley into a four-season destination resort.

◄ A bald eagle soars above a melt pond near Glacier Creek. The Girdwood area supports a large diversity of wildlife. Moose and black bear sometimes roam the community's streets, while mountain goats live in significant numbers on the higher slopes of the upper valley.

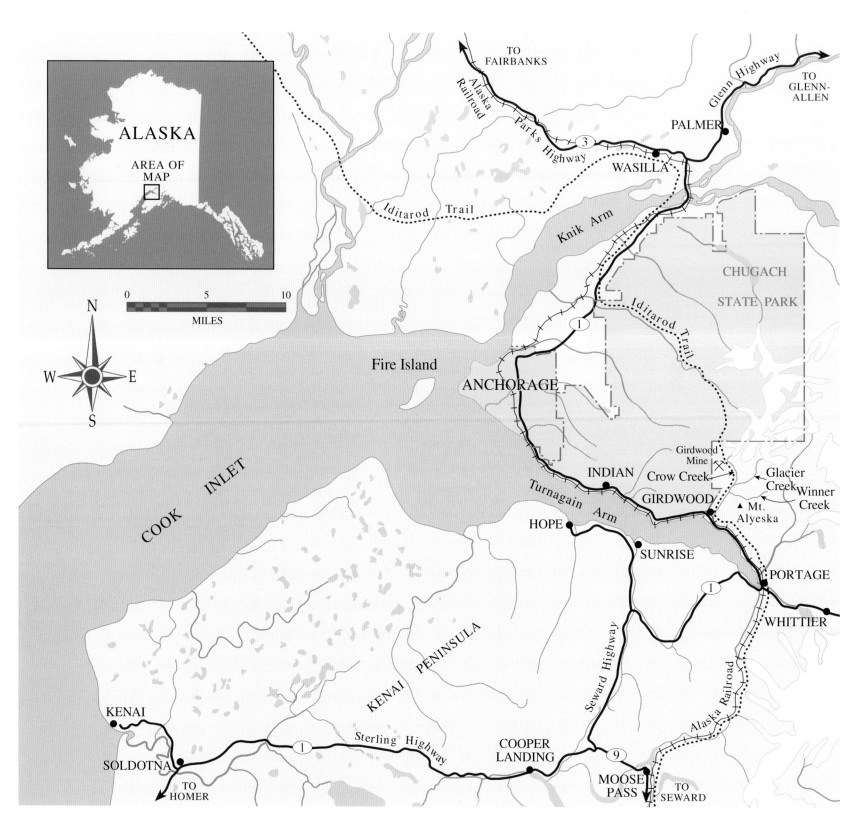

TO
FAIRBANKS

TO
GLENN-
ALLEN

ALASKA

AREA OF
MAP

Glenn Highway

Alaska Railroad

Parks Highway

③

PALMER

WASILLA

Iditarod Trail

N

W   E

S

Knik Arm

CHUGACH

STATE PARK

Iditarod Trail

①

Fire Island

ANCHORAGE

0   5   10

MILES

Girdwood
Mine

Glacier
Creek

Crow Creek

Winner
Creek

COOK   INLET

Turnagain   Arm

INDIAN

GIRDWOOD

▲ Mt.
Alyeska

HOPE

SUNRISE

PORTAGE

①

WHITTIER

KENAI   PENINSULA

Seward Highway

Alaska Railroad

KENAI

Sterling Highway

①

COOPER
LANDING

⑨

SOLDOTNA

TO
HOMER

MOOSE
PASS

TO
SEWARD

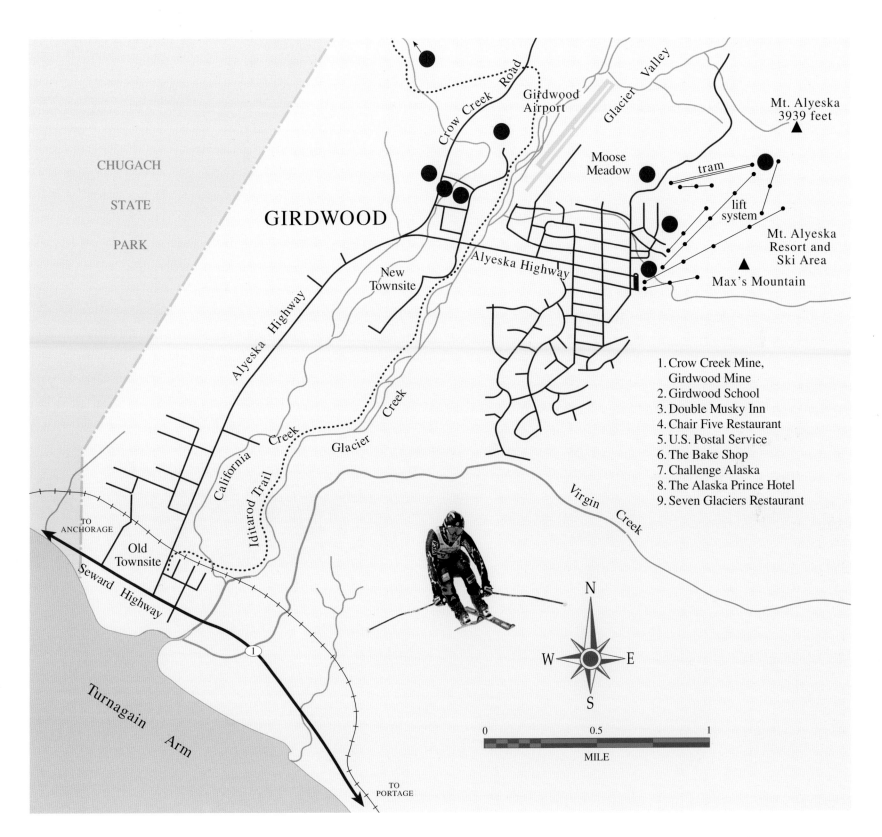

CHUGACH
STATE
PARK

GIRDWOOD

Crow Creek Road

Girdwood Airport

Glacier Valley

Mt. Alyeska
3939 feet ▲

Moose Meadow

tram

lift system

Mt. Alyeska
Resort and
Ski Area ▲

Max's Mountain

Alyeska Highway

New Townsite

Alyeska Highway

California Creek

Iditarod Trail

Glacier Creek

Virgin Creek

1. Crow Creek Mine,
   Girdwood Mine
2. Girdwood School
3. Double Musky Inn
4. Chair Five Restaurant
5. U.S. Postal Service
6. The Bake Shop
7. Challenge Alaska
8. The Alaska Prince Hotel
9. Seven Glaciers Restaurant

TO ANCHORAGE

Old Townsite

Seward Highway

1

Turnagain Arm

N
W   E
S

TO PORTAGE

0   0.5   1
MILE

1
Girdwood's Golden Beginnings

Dreams of gold first brought people to Glacier Valley, including tough men like Chris Spillum, who set off on foot in the winter of 1896 to stake what would become the most productive claims in the valley.

He returned that summer with his partners, the Crow Creek Boys, to recover ten thousand dollars in gold and lay the foundation for a large mining enterprise. It was a hydraulic placer operation, using water to free the metal from gold-bearing, creek-bed deposits called placer. At the height of production, a mile-long flume funneled water from Crow Creek into high-pressure hoses called giants that washed the placer into huge sluice boxes to recover the gold.

Four years later a transplanted Irishman named James Girdwood staked four claims above the Crow Creek Mine and started the second large hydraulic operation in the valley. Girdwood's venture closed in 1908, but the Crow Creek Mine continued to operate for many years, and a later owner, Arne Erickson, eventually turned it into a tourist attraction to save it from demolition.

Smaller operators worked the valley streams and later the mountainsides, where veins of quartz were mined for gold. Many were immigrants from Europe who sought the American dream—people like Joe Danich, Harry Bahrenberg, and Axel Lindblad.

A small community called Glacier City rose near where Glacier Creek flows into Turnagain Arm. Later renamed Girdwood, the little town became a recreation center for the miners and later for railway crews. Five of the sixteen buildings in 1917 were saloons. The town's setting was so scenic that it served as the backdrop for the first movie filmed in Alaska.

The mines closed as World War II broke out, and Girdwood lay dormant until construction of the highway that connected the seaport of Seward with Anchorage—a highway that eventually opened the way to creation of the Alyeska Resort.

◄◄ Early-day miner Chris Spillum gazes through the smoke of his pipe and his cook fire. Spillum came close to death when he made a midwinter dash in 1896 to file the Glacier Valley claims that later became known as Crow Creek Mine. [Anchorage Museum of History and Art]

◄Gus Norton and Bob Griffiths rest their dogs in Girdwood in December 1911 amid a fifty-four-day trip over the Iditarod Trail to haul the first shipment of gold from the Interior Alaska town of Iditarod to the port city of Seward. Wells Fargo hired the well-known mushers to bring out gold valued at $500,000. Thousands of treasure seekers made the five-hundred-mile trek over the Iditarod Trail to the goldfields of the Interior between 1911 and 1925. [Anchorage Museum of History and Art]

James Girdwood

Enterprising Irishman

He was shrewd and handsome with a dynamic personality, as equally at ease with the president of the United States as with the rough men and women who sought fortune in the Last Frontier. His name was James Girdwood, born in 1862 in Belfast, Ireland, one of five sons and six daughters of a justice of the peace and linen merchant and his wife.

Girdwood came to America in 1882 and struck it rich—first in the linen business on the East Coast and then in the goldfields of Alaska. His vision was big and bold, driven by a positive attitude he summarized in a notebook he carried in his pocket. There, in back, were his favorite sayings: "Remember always that American ends in I CAN" and "If your cloud doesn't have a silver lining, turn it inside out."

Somewhere along the way he picked up the title of colonel, even though he never saw military service.

He was friends with President Teddy Roosevelt, the Guggenheims, Goodyear Tire Company magnate Frank Seiberling, and poet Robert Service, among others, and he used his friends and acquaintances to help finance his Alaska ventures. His first prospectus on his gold claims on Crow Creek raised $300,000 on promises of annual returns of $150,000—a figure he would never reach.

Girdwood followed a well-worn path into the gold creeks that line Turnagain Arm, one that dates back to 1848 when the Russian-American Company sent Peter Doroshin, a mining engineer from St. Petersburg, to search for gold around Cook Inlet. Doroshin spent three summers in the area, finding gold along the Kenai River. Forty years later, gold seekers were back. These were prospectors who had worked their way north from the depleted goldfields

in California, through British Columbia, and up the panhandle of Alaska.

The first big strike in this part of Alaska was in 1888 at Hope, on the south side of Turnagain Arm. The Sunrise strike soon followed, then Six-Mile Creek, Mills Creek, and Canyon Creek. The rush was on. Among the thousands of gold seekers who stepped off the boat in the summer of 1896 was James Girdwood, intrigued by the stories spun by his West Coast friends.

Unlike most miners, Girdwood was a man of considerable means by the time he arrived in Turnagain Arm. As a twenty-year-old immigrant in New York City with four hundred dollars in his pocket, he had gone to work as a linen salesman for McCrum, Watson, and Mercer. Twelve years later he controlled more than half of the U.S. market for Irish linens. He sold his business to his associates in 1894.

Alaska became Girdwood's new passion. By 1900, when most prospectors had moved on to Nome's golden beaches or followed the great rush to the Klondike, Girdwood found himself near the head of Crow Creek Valley, where the Goat and Crow glaciers cross paths. He staked four claims—Alpha, Omega, Annex, and Little Gussie—and organized the Crow Creek Hydraulic Mining Company.

Girdwood's claims were relatively rich but fatally flawed. His land was strewn with huge boulders and he had to dump his operation's leftover rocks and gravel—the tailings—into Crow Creek, where they soon interfered with the other large mining project in the valley. Fred Moffitt, a U.S. Geological Survey geologist, visited the site in 1904 and found it "made up of immense boulders and angular blocks, sometimes 10 to 12 feet in diameter, thrown down in great confusion."

Girdwood raised $300,000 to finance the huge hydraulic operation he needed to efficiently work his claims. The prospectus he prepared overstated the return ["$150,000 a year"] and underplayed the challenges ["The boulders are relatively few in number. . . ."]. Seven years into the operation, mine records reported $14,318 in earnings for the year and $14,869 in expenses. Even at the height of the operation, Girdwood took out no more than $106,000 in a year.

By 1906 Girdwood was working two large pits with the high-pressure hoses known as giants. The giants washed dirt, gravel, and rock into sluice boxes, where the gold settled out. A five-ton crane removed rocks too large to move through the sluice boxes.

Working conditions were as daunting as the scale of the equipment. The mining site had few trees to shelter the twenty workers who spent much of their twelve-hour shifts cold and wet. But they earned top wages for the time—five dollars a day plus room and board.

Girdwood's operation was cut short in 1908 when the owners of the Crow Creek Mine went to court to protect their down-creek dam from Girdwood's tailings. The court applied the doctrine of "first in time, first in right," effectively ending large-scale commercial mining in the upper valley. But shrewd businessman that he was, Girdwood managed to gain full title to the claim property in 1906, and his heirs sold it to Anchorage businessman Herb Lang in 1964. Lang subdivided part of the land into thirty cabin sites and sold the remaining property to Gary McCarthy, who operates a gold and gravel business and sells Girdwood's troublesome boulders to Anchorage landscapers.

Ever resourceful, Girdwood was on to other ventures by the time the court ruled against him. When his friends Daniel and Isaac Guggenheim formed the Alaska Syndicate to develop the world's richest copper deposits at Kennicott, Alaska, Girdwood bought his own copper claims in Prince William Sound. He formed the LaTouche Copper Mining Company in 1907, with himself as president owning 1,666 shares, adventurer Paul Niedieck with 1,000 shares, and Valdez resident George Barrack with 334 shares.

Niedieck was one of the many colorful people

▲ James Girdwood washes gold-bearing gravel outside his cabin on upper Crow Creek. He wrote his family that the cabin was "comfortable and dry." [CITY OF GIRDWOOD]

◄ James Girdwood chats with friends outside his cabin in the community of Girdwood in 1925 or 1926. Girdwood bought four lots from the federal government in 1923 for fifteen dollars each. [GIRDWOOD FAMILY]

▲ A steely-eyed statue of James Cook gazes upon Cook Inlet from a pedestal in Anchorage. The great English navigator named the inlet's Turnagain Arm in frustration in 1778 when land blocked his way as he searched for the Northwest Passage. His ships had to "turn again" to retrace their way out. Girdwood and Glacier Valley front on Turnagain Arm.

▶ The natural phenomenon known as a bore tide riles the waters of Turnagain Arm. The great variance between low and high tide, and the narrow, shallow sloping of the Arm, create the rapidly rising rushes of tidal water. Bore tides in Turnagain Arm range from two to six feet in height, traveling between ten and fifteen miles an hour.

who floated through Girdwood's life. A German naturalist and big-game hunter, Niedieck set off at the turn of the century on an eight-year-long hunting trip, including a year and a half in Alaska where he invested in mining claims. He turned his adventures into a best-selling book, *With Rifle on Five Continents.*

The new company bought Barrack's copper claims on LaTouche Island along with four others and hired Barrack as superintendent. The Crow Creek gold operation became a subsidiary. LaTouche sold its copper interests in 1915 to a company purchased by the Guggenheims a decade later. When the Guggenheim company tried to work Girdwood's claims, it found "the ore was badly faulted, the ground was heavy and the nature of the ore made the mining recovery low."

Girdwood continued to summer in Alaska, working his gold claims and visiting with his neighbors. When he first arrived in the late 1890s, the little town on the banks of Turnagain Arm was known as Glacier City and consisted of one main street, several small log cabins, and a line of tent frames. By 1907 the community had a new name and its first post office. According to Alaska historian Robert DeArmond, "Girdwood was widely known among the miners and was so well regarded by them that they named the little camp for him."

Placer mining fueled Glacier Valley's first gold rush, lode mining its second. The *Seward Weekly Gateway* reported a new Crow Creek strike in July 1921, with gold-bearing quartz valued at a hundred dollars a ton. By September the rush was on, reinvigorating the town of Girdwood for a short time, and kindling new dreams for Girdwood the man. James Girdwood told the *Seattle Post Dispatch* in 1925 that he would have his mines in full production by 1926.

It was not to be. Although he ordered machines and equipment, he became ill and died in March 1928 at the New Jersey estate he called Clonaver, named for the street in Ireland where his family lived.

The Chugach Mountains

The Chugach Mountain Range above Girdwood stretches 250 miles from Turnagain Arm on the west to Bering Glacier near Cordova on the east, in a band 60 miles wide. The range includes most of the 5.6-million-acre Chugach National Forest. This photo, taken along the Seward Highway between Anchorage and Girdwood, looks east over the range and its hundreds of mostly unnamed peaks.

The mountains surrounding Girdwood went on an epic journey before settling down in a 250-mile swath across Alaska from Anchorage to Valdez and points east.

Geologists say the rocks that make up the Chugach Mountain Range caught a ride on the Pacific plate, a mammoth portion of the Earth's crust that meets the North American plate in Alaska. The trip took millions of years.

The Chugach rocks collided with the North American plate in what is now Southcentral Alaska, resulting in the gradual uplift of the Chugach Range. Today, the older Chugach rocks are found inland while the relatively younger rocks hug the coastline.

As many as fifty large pieces of the earth's crust came together to form the state of Alaska. The pieces arrived in waves over the ages, with the last large one arriving about 200 million years ago. The building process continues today.

20

The First People

The first humans came to Cook Inlet more than five thousand years ago, but it was the Dena'ina Indians who stayed and made the area their home.

The Dena'ina, who are also called the Tanaina, migrated into the region around A.D. 500, spreading out over 41,000 square miles around Cook Inlet, west to Lake Clark, north through the Susitna and Matanuska River drainages, and south to the Kenai Mountains. They encountered coastal Eskimos on their southern range, and their name for Ninilchik on the lower Kenai Peninsula translates to "lodge is built on other people's lands."

More than many aboriginal populations, the Dena'ina lived a migratory existence, harvesting nature's bounty. They named most places and natural features so they could pass down the location of food sources and other items used in their survival and travel. Almost every waterway and peak along Turnagain Arm had a Dena'ina name except for Glacier Valley and its creeks and mountains.

Both the Dena'ina and the coast Eskimos in this area, known as the Alutiiq, were decimated by a series of epidemics beginning in the 1830s after their initial contact with Europeans.

Today the Dena'ina number some nine hundred people, of whom about seventy-five retain their original language. Many of them are shareholders in Cook Inlet Region Inc., one of the Native regional business corporations created in 1971 to help settle Native land claims. An estimated three thousand Alutiiq live on the Kenai Peninsula, Prince William Sound, and Kodiak, with about four hundred still speaking their native language. Most are shareholders in Koniag Inc. or Chugach Alaska Corp., two other Native corporations.

▲ The brief nights of summer create spectacular sunsets along Turnagain Arm. At summer solstice, the area enjoys more than nineteen hours of daylight as the sun rises at 3:21 a.m. and sets at 10:42 p.m. The Dena'ina harvested beluga whale, salmon and hooligan, a form of smelt, from the arm.

◄ Members of a Dena'ina Indian family pose near their summer quarters in the Seldovia area near lower Cook Inlet in 1901. Archaeological research indicates that the Dena'ina migrated into the Cook Inlet area about fifteen hundred years ago. This southerly migration eventually met up with a culture of coastal Eskimos, known as the Alutiiq. [ANCHORAGE MUSEUM OF HISTORY AND ART]

Axel Lindblad

Some men are bigger than life—such as Axel Lindblad, longtime caretaker of James Girdwood's Crow Creek mining claims.

A large Swede who fought in the Boer War in South Africa at the turn of the twentieth century, Lindblad came to Alaska in search of gold but ended up mushing a dog team between Seward and Sunrise, carrying the mail. He froze both hands during a spring flood and lost all the fingers on his right hand and all but his thumb and index finger on his left hand. While he was in the hospital recovering, he had a doctor cut a slot deep in his right hand where he could place a knife so that he could continue cutting wood and doing his own skinning of animal pelts.

Lindblad spent many years in the Girdwood area, working gold claims during the summer, trapping in the winter, and building a series of cabins. He remained a worthy opponent who once chased a man to Seward after losing part of his ear during a fight.

In March 1923 while Lindblad was on a trip to Anchorage, an avalanche destroyed several of the buildings at the Girdwood mine, where he resided. "It's very fortunate I wasn't up there at the time as I think I would not have had one chance in a thousand to get out unhurt," he later wrote.

In the 1950s, Arne Erickson dictated the story of Lindblad's life to his granddaughter and recalled the Swede's final days in the late 1940s. "He had cancer and went to many doctors in Anchorage. The Crow Creek people raised $700 to send him outside [Alaska]. He returned feeling much better but towards the end of the summer he got hot and sweaty and then chilled while climbing up to an old cabin where he wanted to salvage the metal roof. He died in an Anchorage hospital. He was in his sixties."

Axel Lindblad displays beaver pelts he trapped in 1947. The Swedish immigrant, who lost eight fingers to frostbite, led an adventurous life in Glacier Valley for many years as gold miner and trapper. [CITY OF GIRDWOOD]

Crow Creek Mine

On a frigid January 1, 1896, Chris Spillum walked around the head of Turnagain Arm to stake claims on Crow Creek more than thirty miles away. Deep snow and extreme temperatures almost killed him, but his gamble paid off. Spillum ended up with the most productive claims in Glacier Valley.

Spillum and his partners, known as the Crow Creek Boys, spent their first summer proving up the claims and whipsawing lumber for flumes, sluice boxes, and a bunkhouse. They reportedly took out ten thousand dollars at season's end. The next summer they hired men at five dollars a day to begin building a road from the beach to the claims.

One of the partners, Charles Brooks, a lawyer from Sunrise, sold his interest in the operation to Sam Wible in 1899. Wible, a mining engineer, had come to California during the 1849 gold rush. Wible laid out the lines for the hydraulic works that washed massive amounts of gravel through sluice boxes to uncover the gold. By then the operation had forty-three employees.

Spillum's crew dammed Crow Creek above their workings, diverting the stream by ditch and pipeline and laying bare the creek bed for sluicing. They used high-pressure hoses to work deposits as much as 250 feet deep and eventually sluiced more than 1,000 feet along the creek.

The scale was massive. The flume that built up water pressure for the giant hoses was a mile long. The sluice boxes, measuring twelve feet long and four to five feet square, were placed end-to-end, forming one sluice between fifty and one hundred feet in length. In the sluice, the gold—heavier than the gravel from the creek bed—settled out of the water as it ran over a series of wood ridges, called riffles.

The Crow Creek Boys, incorporated as the Crow Creek Consolidated Mining Company, sold out to the Nutter brothers and R. D. Dawson in 1907. They operated as the Nutter-Dawson Company until 1912, when they incorporated as the Crow Creek Gold Mining Company.

Over its years of operation, Crow Creek Mine yielded a total of forty-five thousand ounces of gold.

The original mess hall, with its Lang cooking stove and cooking utensils, still stands at the Crow Creek Mine. Six of the original fifteen buildings constructed between 1898 and 1906 remain. Up to thirty workers lived in the camp, which used hydraulic works to recover placer gold, which is gold freed from the mother rock by glaciers and water erosion and concentrated in the sands and gravels of stream beds.

Arne Erickson

He left a legacy much richer than the gold he sought: Crow Creek Mine, a snapshot of history almost perfectly preserved at mile 3.5 on the Crow Creek Road.

Arne Erickson arrived in Alaska in 1910, a young man from Norway with a bad case of gold fever. He had no claims of his own so he worked for other miners—three years in Fairbanks and then on to Flat, where his luck didn't improve. So he decided to check out the Turnagain area.

In 1922, Erickson was hired by the Nutter brothers to supervise operations at their Crow Creek Mine, the operation originally developed by Chris Spillum and the Crow Creek Boys. Erickson leased three claims from the owners in 1923, and he worked for shares when John Holmgren bought the mine in 1925.

Erickson acquired the deed to the property in 1933 and continued to operate the mine until 1938, when labor costs almost equaled production costs. At the height of his operation, he took out forty thousand dollars in gold in a single year.

Erickson's application for a patent, or title, to the land was denied in 1960 based on findings of a mining engineer who declared the claim worthless. The federal government then voided the mineral survey that had allowed him to mine the claims. He was left with only three acres, the buildings, and the machinery.

Crow Creek Mine reopened in 1967 under a federal permit stipulating that access to the now-historic mine site remain open to the public. Erickson and his wife, Cleora, stayed on. They lived in Anchorage during the winter but drove their old DeSoto to the mine in the summer, showing tourists how to pan for gold and flying the Norwegian flag from one of the old cabins.

Erickson later sold the mine to Cynthia and Barney Toohey, and the property was added to the National Register of Historic Places in 1980. The Tooheys straightened out the boundary issues involving the mine through a land swap of property they owned near Seward. Today the family owns fifty-four acres surrounding the site.

▲ Cynthia Toohey owns this 2.5-ounce gold nugget found at her mine on Crow Creek. The largest nugget found at the mine weighed 4 ounces.

▶ Arne Erickson with Cynthia Toohey

[CYNTHIA TOOHEY]

Cynthia Toohey

When Barney Toohey lay dying of cancer, forty-five neighbors showed up at Crow Creek Mine to sing Christmas carols to the engaging man they had grown to love. It was the kind of gesture that reinforced Cynthia Toohey's decision to move her family to the old mining camp, where there was no phone, no electricity, no running water.

The family of five, then four after Barney's death in 1982, mostly lived in one room, in an 1898 cabin the Tooheys fixed up after acquiring Crow Creek Mine, the largest gold camp on Crow Creek. They restored most of the buildings and shared the property with visitors during the summer. Cynthia liked to say they mined the tourists during the summer and mined the creek the rest of the year.

Crow Creek Mine was a strange destination for a street-savvy New York City native, but anyone who knows Cynthia understands that she moves to her own drummer. She arrived in Anchorage at the age of twenty-three, not knowing a soul, "to find a husband." She went to work for Reeve Aleutian Airways, an unconventional airline that serviced an area known for its foul weather.

She met Barney in a bar in Talkeetna, on a road trip with Roberta Reeve Sheldon. He was fresh off the boat with a job as an engineer on a survey crew. "He was just a handsome guy, a big, tall, black-haired Irishman," she once told a reporter. "Six-foot-four. I was skinny and cute back then. We started going out right then and there. It was one of those great romances."

They married two years later, moved around a bit, and returned to Anchorage in 1967, the year that mine owner Arne Erickson first took them to the Crow Creek Mine. They took over the operation Erickson had cultivated for fifty years, first as a gold mine and then as a tourist attraction.

When Erickson died, she buried his ashes in her flower beds at the mine, along with those of the father she adored, and the husband she loved.

"This is my life. This is my home. I'll never leave this state, ever," she told a reporter. "I'm going in the flower bed with the rest of my family."

▲ Cynthia Toohey

◄ Early snow and beautiful fall colors signal the end of the tourist season at Crow Creek Mine. Crow Mountain rises 5,900 feet in the background, the highest peak in Glacier Valley.

25

The Hard-Rock Miners

The street names at the entrance to the valley stand as testament to Girdwood's second gold rush: Monarch, Brenner, Gunnysack, Hottentot. These were hard-rock mines—difficult to operate, almost impossible to reach.

The *Seward Weekly Gateway* reported a find of gold-bearing quartz on July 1, 1921, valued at one hundred dollars a ton. A new gold rush followed in September, and the town of Girdwood, which had dwindled to a few families, boomed again.

The largest and oldest of the lode mines was the Monarch in the upper Crow Creek Valley, discovered in 1909 by Conrad Hores. Anchorage investors purchased the mine in the early 1920s and Harry Staser acquired it at the end of the decade.

Certain that he had discovered his Eldorado,

▲ A turn-of-the-century prospector in upper Crow Creek tests the gold content of that day's mining operation. The Cook Inlet region produced an estimated $6.6 million in gold during the period 1895-1915—not an impressive figure compared with the Fairbanks area, where miners took more than $65 million worth in a single year, 1915. [CITY OF GIRDWOOD]

▶ The buildings of the Monarch Mine stand high in the upper Crow Creek Valley. Longtime owner Harry Staser built bunkhouses, a mess hall, blacksmith shop, powder magazines, and mill buildings at the gold mine in the 1930s. Not much was left by the time this photo was taken in 1949 except the remains of the mill building. [HIBBS FAMILY]

Staser worked a crew of six, giving them a daily pep talk. "Hell, boys," he would say, "there's a million bucks in there and we're gonna get it all out." It didn't work out that way, but he did recover enough gold to pay off his original ten-thousand-dollar investment.

Staser, also a deputy U.S. marshal and a representative in the 1923 and 1925 territorial legislatures, once drove a stage over the Richardson Highway. He died in 1940 when he suffered a heart attack as he attempted to make his way up the precipitous slope to the mine. Joe Danich tried to reopen the Monarch after World War II but the equipment was too run-down and the price of gold too low.

A tram connected the Monarch Mine with the nearby Jewel Mine, which was wiped out by an avalanche in the late 1920s after its owners installed a mill and spent eighty thousand dollars in development.

Just south of the Monarch, Clyde Brenner operated the Brenner Prospect, which included the Gunnysack and consisted of two veins at creek level. Brenner dug tunnels slanting upward through the outcropping of the veins. He worked the operation in the 1920s and '30s, installing a three-stamp mill to extract gold from the quartz.

Henry Bahrenberg built a cabin at Raven Glacier in 1926 on the old Treasure Box claim that he renamed Hottentot. He worked his claims at the Hottentot, near the headwaters of Crow Creek, for twenty years. Bahrenberg was a good friend of Brenner's until the two parted ways over a mining dispute.

Bahrenburg's lode mine was called "the crudest operation ever seen," with one tunnel into the west side of Jewel Mountain and another in a craggy rock face near Raven Glacier. Never able to afford a proper stamp mill, Bahrenberg rolled large boulders over his ore to break down the gold-laden quartz. He stashed his gold concentrate in burlap ore bags and used a windlass to move them down to the valley floor. But he earned a reputation as a good cook who was known for his fluffy sourdough bread and mouthwatering roasted beaver.

▲ Passengers and crew of the *Alaska* attempt to open a channel through the ice during the boat's inaugural trip to Girdwood in 1912. The *Alaska* was one of three small boats that hauled miners and equipment around Turnagain Arm, which was too shallow for larger vessels. [ANCHORAGE MUSEUM OF HISTORY AND ART]

▲ Next to gold, the most precious possession at the turn of the twentieth century was a horse. These two horses, Maude and Lillian, worked throughout the Girdwood area. [CITY OF GIRDWOOD]

Early Girdwood

► The little town of Girdwood, with about sixty permanent residents, lies beneath the winter snows of 1917. Temperatures that winter fell to a rare minus-sixty degrees. An unnamed peak that locals call Pyramid rises behind the community. Most of the area's timber was cut for mining and construction purposes. [CITY OF GIRDWOOD]

▼ Surveyors from the Alaska Engineering Commission take readings as they lay out a regular street pattern for Girdwood in 1916. The commission assigned street names such as Dawson Avenue, Gold Street, and Easy Street. [ANCHORAGE MUSEUM OF HISTORY AND ART]

Girdwood was a community born of convenience just before the turn of the twentieth century to supply bed, food, and drink to travelers and miners.

Girdwood's strategic location on Turnagain Arm at the entrance to Glacier Valley made it a natural supply point and road stop. Small craft delivered goods and people during the warmer months, and by 1910 a well-developed trail linked Girdwood with the northern terminus of the Alaska Northern Railway. Two major overland trails also led to Girdwood, including the Iditarod, which began in Seward and ended in Nome. The other route hugged Turnagain Arm to Indian, where it headed over the mountains and into the Anchorage area.

Kenneth Gideon, an engineering student at the University of Washington, visited the community in 1913 and had the following to report:

"The cluster of log buildings that made up the place housed much more interesting specimens than could be found in the woods surrounding the place. These old-timers had come there when the old Alaska Northern railroad was being built. It was just a few miles past the end of steel and had been chosen as a site for a sawmill to cut ties for the railroad. The latter went on the rocks and Girdwood lay down and died.

"When we came there, its one street of false fronts and boarded-up windows looked like a deserted movie setting."

The community perked up during construction of the Alaska Railroad from 1915 to 1923, remained vibrant through the modest gold rush of the 1920s, and came to life again during construction of the Seward Highway, which was completed in 1951.

The town more than doubled in size during the 1980s, then doubled again in the 1990s. About 2,500 people now call Girdwood home.

◄ The seven daughters of Joe Reno and his wife made up the total school population of Girdwood in 1916. Later the Estes family added five boys to the one-room school. Joe Reno chaired the school board, which hired the teacher, typically a young woman who stayed in the job for one year. The Reno family operated the local general store. [CITY OF GIRDWOOD]

◄ Customers in the early 1920s gather at the Girdwood bar that went through a number of name changes before Joe Danich bought it in 1939 and named it the Little Dipper. The building had fourteen rooms upstairs, and a kitchen, bar, restaurant, post office, and liquor store on the main level. [CITY OF GIRDWOOD]

The Alaska Railroad

An Alaska Railroad construction crew works on the trestle crossing Bird Creek, twelve miles north of Girdwood, around 1916. Two sawmills at Girdwood produced ties and timber for railroad construction, which took eight years to complete.

[ANCHORAGE MUSEUM OF HISTORY AND ART]

It was the first great federal project in Alaska—the 470-mile Alaska Railroad that links together Alaska's major population centers, including Seward, Anchorage, and Fairbanks. For the little town of Girdwood, it meant year-round transportation, jobs for local residents, and mail on a daily basis.

The railroad is the northernmost in North America and for decades was the only one owned by the federal government. The railroad's roots date back to 1903 when Alaska Central Railway built the first railroad in Alaska, starting in Seward and extending fifty miles north. The company filed for bankruptcy in 1907 and reorganized as Alaska Northern Railway Company, extending the railroad

to Kern Creek, seventy-one miles from Seward and just four miles from Girdwood.

In 1912, Congress appointed a commission to study transportation problems in Alaska and two years later agreed to fund construction and operation of a railroad to "connect open harbors on the southern coast of Alaska" with the Interior. Construction was estimated to cost $35 million.

The Alaska Engineering Commission surveyed railroad routes in 1914 and President Woodrow Wilson selected a route from Seward north to the Tanana River with branch lines to the Matanuska coalfields. The main line was later extended to Fairbanks. The commission laid out an ambitious street pattern for Girdwood in 1916, with names such as Dawson Street, Gold Street, and Easy Street.

Actual construction started in 1915 and a tent city of 2,000 people sprang up on the banks of Ship Creek when the railroad moved its headquarters from Seward to what would become Anchorage. By 1917 some 4,500 people were working on the railroad, which was completed in 1923 when President Warren Harding drove the golden spike. The federal government sold the railroad to the state of Alaska in 1985 for $22.3 million.

A snowplow-equipped locomotive clears track south of Girdwood in 1912. The Alaska Northern Railway came within four miles of Girdwood before it ran out of money in 1915. The federal government later purchased the railroad and this locomotive became ARR [Alaska Railroad] #1.
[ANCHORAGE MUSEUM OF HISTORY AND ART]

"The Chechahcos"

The Girdwood area, down to Portage Glacier, was the setting in 1924 for *The Chechahcos*, the first feature movie filmed entirely in Alaska. Austin "Cap" Lathrop, Alaska's first homegrown millionaire, financed the silent film, which featured art titles by Sydney Laurence, Alaska's most famous painter.

The film tells the story of two good-hearted prospectors who take in a young girl, apparently left motherless after a ship explosion. As the miners strike it rich, the younger prospector falls in love with their ward. All learn through hard experience that disreputable gamblers can be as dangerous as the frozen north. A collapsing glacier kills the gambler villain, and mother and daughter are reunited.

The melodrama provides ample excuses for showing off the Alaska landscape in sled dog chases, hazardous whitewater crossings, and glacier rescues.

When released in New York, *Variety* dismissed the plot as "hokey." The trade publication doubted if any film with such an unpronounceable title—it means newcomer to the north—could be a commercial success "even in summer when snow and ice stuff are such a welcome relief." *The Chechahcos* failed in the Lower 48 states and dropped from movie history.

The movie starred William Dills as Horseshoe Riley, Albert Van Antwerp as Bob Dexter, Eva Gordon as Mrs. Stanlaw, Alexis Luce as Richard Steele, Gladys Johnson as Ruth Stanlaw, and Guerney Hays as Pierre. A 35 mm print of the movie and a 16 mm reduction print reside in the Alaska Film Archives at the University of Alaska Fairbanks.

▲ Eva Gordon and Alexis Luce stand on the shores of Turnagain Arm in this scene from *The Chechahcos*. [ANCHORAGE MUSEUM OF HISTORY AND ART]

▶ The cast of the silent movie *The Chechahcos* gathers on the main street of Girdwood. The film, shot mainly in the Girdwood area, featured a mostly Alaskan cast and art titles by Sydney Laurence, Alaska's most famous oil painter. [ANCHORAGE MUSEUM OF HISTORY AND ART]

Austin "Cap" Lathrop

A ninth-grade dropout who gambled his future on a small boat in Alaska grew to become Alaska's first self-made millionaire and the most powerful person in the territory.

Austin "Cap" Lathrop was born in Lapeer, Michigan, made his first fortune as a street grader in Anacortes, Washington, and then lost it all in the financial Panic of 1883. He talked his way into a bank loan and purchased half of the two-masted schooner L.J. Perry, which he brought to Alaska in 1895.

Lathrop became a welcome sight along Turnagain Arm, where he hauled miners, mail, and freight and became known as Cap, short for Captain. "Anyone who operated anything that could float was called Cap," he would later recall.

And he made money—enough money that he could drill a commercial oil well. This venture fell victim to federal land withdrawals designed to curb the economic ambitions of the Guggenheims and their Alaska Syndicate. President Teddy Roosevelt designated twenty-three million acres of land in Southcentral Alaska as the Chugach National Forest in 1907 to stop the Syndicate from developing coal-fields in the Cordova area and mining operations in other parts of Prince William Sound.

Lathrop ventured into entertainment, building the Empress Theatre in Anchorage in 1915 and other theaters in Valdez, Cordova, and Fairbanks. He eventually constructed his dream, the Fourth Avenue Theater in Anchorage, and financed *The Chechahcos*, set in Girdwood, the first feature movie shot in Alaska.

By the mid-1930s, "Lathrop owned most things worth owning—a bank, apartment buildings, movie theaters, the Healy Coal Mine, the *Fairbanks Daily News-Miner* and a beer distributorship that netted him a nickel on every bottle of Olympia shipped from Seattle," wrote Alaska publisher Bob Atwood in his autobiography.

Two giant personalities, Lathrop and Atwood clashed from the beginning. "A real muscle guy with a horn of a voice," Atwood wrote. "A fierce Republican . . . frontier wise and steely eyed at age seventy." Lathrop opposed construction of the Alaska Highway, statehood, and airmail service, all things dear to Atwood's heart.

Only months from his eighty-fifth birthday, Lathrop was struck by a coal car in a railroad yard near his Healy Coal Mine and died on July 26, 1950.

▲ President Teddy Roosevelt created the Chugach National Forest in 1907 to stop the Alaska Syndicate, owned by Eastern industrialists J.P. Morgan and the Guggenheims, from further development in the Prince William Sound area. The national forest designation ended Cap Lathrop's oil exploration plans.

◄ Austin "Cap" Lathrop

[ANCHORAGE MUSEUM OF HISTORY AND ART]

The Seward Highway

The Seward Highway traverses the base of an unnamed peak about four miles south of Girdwood. The highway, completed in 1951, links Girdwood with Anchorage to the north and with the Kenai Peninsula and Seward to the south.

Today it's best known for its unparalleled views, but the Seward Highway owes its existence to the military's desire to have a land link between the major seaport of Seward and the military installations around Anchorage.

Construction of the Seward Highway started in April 1949 at the beginning of the Cold War, financed by federal dollars. The project ignited a spark of economic life in Girdwood that lasted until the ribbon-cutting ceremony on October 19, 1951, and the completed highway set the stage for later resort development.

Girdwood bar owner and community leader Joe Danich recalled, "After the bustle of construction the population plummeted. With the departure of construction families, one child had to be 'imported' for the one-room school to open."

Driving the highway remained a white-knuckle experience until Anchorage's bid for the 1992 and 1994 Winter Olympics prompted a series of upgrades that continues today. Much of the work reduced the avalanche danger on the highway, which avalanche forecaster Dave Hamre called one of the most dangerous roadways in North America.

This safer highway remains among the world's most beautiful drives. A national conservation organization, Scenic America, judged it "America's Most Outstanding Scenic Byway." *National Geographic* called it one of the top ten drives in North America.

The highway is named for William Seward, Abraham Lincoln's secretary of state, who negotiated the purchase of Alaska from Russia in 1867 at a price of about two cents an acre.

Joe Danich

Joe Danich came seeking gold but ended up revitalizing a floundering community.

A native of Yugoslavia, Danich arrived in Alaska in 1935, prospecting during the winter months and working for the Alaska Road Commission on the Anchorage-Palmer highway during the summer. He discovered coal near Moose Creek and used proceeds from the sale of the Buffalo Coal Mine to purchase the Big Dipper Bar in Anchorage.

Anchorage quickly grew too big for Danich's liking so he and his wife, Alice, moved to Girdwood in 1939, where they bought the Glacier Bar and renamed it the Little Dipper: "Customers wanted, no experience necessary." He acquired the Jewel and Monarch Mines, which he worked during the summers, along with plucking ducks for miners for three cents each and doing their laundry.

The Little Dipper turned into the social and technology center for the community. It had the town's first indoor toilet and first telephone, and for many years it was the only place with electricity. Danich was a founding member of the Alyeska Ski Corp. and was the first mayor of Girdwood after it became an incorporated city in 1961.

A pilot who flew a 65-horsepower airplane and often delivered payrolls to mine managers, Danich built a fifteen-hundred-foot airstrip on land he owned on the Turnagain Arm side of the highway. The Territory of Alaska paid him $1,500 for the facility. When the airstrip sank during the 1964 earthquake, the State of Alaska returned the land, tidewater and all, to Danich.

The Little Dipper burned during the earthquake and the Daniches' newly furnished house was flooded with nearly two feet of water. After the quake-damaged highway was rebuilt, Danich oper- ated a gas station at the corner of Seward Highway and Alyeska Highway until 1972, when Alice died and Danich returned to his homeland.

◄ Joe Danich [DALLAS PITZER]

◄ The Little Dipper roadhouse, originally built in the 1910s, became the social center of the community after Joe and Alice Danich bought it in 1939. The Girdwood Community Club held its dances, barbecues, and movie nights there and the post office occupied part of the ground floor. [CITY OF GIRDWOOD]

2

The French Connection

Girdwood's outlook was bleak when the first skiers showed up in the early 1950s to convince the handful of residents that their economic future was tied to the mountain that dominated the end of their valley.

Eleven families, including the Bursiels and the Hibbses, pooled their resources to purchase land at the base of the peak they named Alyeska and begin development of a ski resort. When funds ran out, the group went in search of a benefactor.

They found him in the form of François de Gunzburg, a genuine French baron with a passion for skiing and an interest in Alaska. The baron pronounced the mountain worthy of international development and raised enough money to clear trails, install a mile-long chairlift, and build a day lodge.

To promote his investment, he and his manager, Jim Branch, brought Penny Pitou and Betsy Snite, stars of the Squaw Valley Winter Olympics, for a visit to Alyeska. And they convinced the nation that Alyeska could host the 1963 National Alpine Championships and Olympic trials.

Money was always short, so de Gunzburg and Branch obtained 233 acres of state-leased land adjacent to the resort, which they subdivided and sold for development or bartered in exchange for needed goods and services. A handful of chalets arose in the valley, along with a new business, the Double Musky, which would grow into an internationally acclaimed Cajun restaurant.

New skiers came and stayed—people like Loverne Bercee, the valley historian.

The Good Friday earthquake brought change of a different kind to the valley. Skiing had stopped for the day when the huge temblor hit in 1964, stranding Georgia Pitzer and sixteen others in a tiny cabin for eight days. In Anchorage, John Trautner, who would become one of Girdwood's leading philanthropists, administered first aid to quake victims from the back of his car.

The town at the edge of Turnagain Arm had to be abandoned after the earthquake caused the land to drop an average of seven feet and the area flooded at high tide. Residents picked up the major buildings and moved them and themselves two and a half miles up the valley to what's called the New Girdwood Townsite. There they began a new era that centered around Mount Alyeska.

◄ ◄ The Roundhouse warmup shelter stands above the clouds on Mount Alyeska in this photo from 1962. The Roundhouse, upper terminus of the first chairlift, is being converted into a ski museum. [Steve McCutcheon]

◄ Three skiers in the early 1960s, clad in the gear of that day, prepare to enjoy an Alyeska run. By then, skiers could take advantage of the area's first chairlift.

[Alyeska Resort]

François de Gunzburg

The Baron

Alaskans called him Frenchy: François de Gunzburg, tall, handsome, jovial, unpretentious—just the sort of person who felt at ease in what early resident Virginia Bursiel called "erotic, gregarious Girdwood."

He was also a baron, a member of the Rothschild banking family, who lived in a Paris mansion given to his people generations ago by a French king.

He was the catch of a lifetime for the valley residents who had passed the hat to raise money for land to build a ski resort. He took over their fledgling Alyeska Ski Corp. and invested enough money to turn a rope tow into the beginnings of an international resort that today provides hundreds of year-round jobs.

When de Gunzburg died in 1984, Anchorage publisher Bob Atwood summarized the baron's importance to Alaska: "His was Alaska's first sizeable private investment in a commercial recreation facility. His investment captured the imagination of newspaper and magazine writers throughout the nation. They presented Alaska widely as a new place to invest in new projects."

De Gunzburg's route began in 1949–1950. Valley residents wanted a school, and under territorial rules, the government would supply a teacher if the community provided the school. Locals organized the Girdwood Community Club and built the first school using money collected from showing movies at the local roadhouse.

Part social, part civic, the Girdwood Community Club kept the roads plowed and the light plant operating. It hosted the Christmas parties and the Easter egg hunts. It held raffles and bake sales. It found a way to construct a fire hall and a community center—and to use a special mountain to secure their future.

When the Seward Highway opened in 1951, a group of die-hard skiers came to Girdwood to talk up the area's potential. It was a new concept for the locals, recalled Connie Hibbs, whose family moved to the valley that year: "Skiing was not part of our vocabulary back then."

"Ernie Baumann used to come to our house and talk with the men," Hibbs said. "He had fallen in love with the mountain and felt it needed to be developed. He got everyone hot to do something about it."

Baumann and fellow skiers Sven Johanson—Alaska's only Winter Olympian at the time—and Joe Gayman drew up a development plan and filed to get the federal government to sell off 160 acres at the mountain's base and lower elevations. Girdwood residents asked to join in, but Baumann said no. "They wanted to do it themselves," Virginia Bursiel said.

When Baumann "couldn't beg or borrow the down payment," the Girdwood Community Club stepped in, formed a nonprofit corporation—Alyeska Ski Corp.—and collected enough money to embark on a development program that would give the organization patent [title] to the land. Alyeska Ski Corp. ended its first year with $196.99 in the bank.

The group brought in new directors and reorganized as a for-profit group in 1957, authorized to sell $275,000 in stock. The group's prospectus boldly stated that "expert skiers from areas such as Alta, Aspen, Sun Valley and Squaw Valley have skied this area and rank its potential equal to any of the Stateside areas." It laid out a three-year plan to install two rope tows, a chairlift, and day lodge, and listed several first-year achievements: "road into the area, installation of a 1,300-foot rope tow and sub floor for a 32'x36' warm-up hut."

It was the height of the Cold War and the community's civil defense director, Joe Danich, was charged with building an 850-vehicle parking lot in Girdwood as an evacuation area for Anchorage in the event of attack. The federal government provided a bulldozer, which Danich and Bob Bursiel used to push through a primitive road to Mount Alyeska, building what Virginia Bursiel described as "very rough wooden bridges" over the streams.

The corporation's dollar-a-share stock brought in several thousand dollars but it wasn't enough. The money ran out, and Frances Richins Clark hit the road, looking for new investors.

Clark was the wife of an FBI agent who was a friend of Danich, by then president of the ski corporation. The corporation brought Frances Clark in as a director and agent who would sell its stock. A vivacious redhead, Clark had an almost uncanny knack for raising money for worthy but impoverished causes.

Clark made two lengthy trips on behalf of the struggling corporation, traveling coast to coast and talking with everyone who was anyone in the world of American skiing. Her mission eventually ended in Aspen, where she met de Gunzburg, an ardent skier whose Denver-based oil company owned a number of mineral leases in Alaska. It was a historic moment, as several of the original Girdwood investors wrote in a letter to *The Anchorage Times:*

"It was Mrs. Clark, ignoring the singular lack of response among her Anchorage neighbors, who traveled the width and depth of the 48 states in an intensive, exhausting and often morale-bleeding sales tour that culminated in bringing Alyeska's attention to de Gunzburg and other stockholders of his Owanah Oil Company. . . . Owanah's investment in Girdwood . . . converted the ski area from potential to reality but it was Mrs. Clark's remarkable vitality and inspired promotion that made that investment possible."

For de Gunzburg, it was love at first sight. He hiked up Mount Alyeska to check out the terrain, escorted by Jon Domela of the newly organized ski patrol, Gary King of Gary King's Ski School, and ski instructors Joe Young and Gary Lyons. The group then helicoptered to the top and took an exhilarating run down. De Gunzburg proclaimed the mountain "a skiing resource of international patronage."

The mountain became "his plaything," said Virginia Bursiel. De Gunzburg raised money from his own company and from Laurence Rockefeller of New York City, Seagram's board chairman Samuel Bronfman, Texas hotel magnate T. L. Wynne Jr., and a couple of Texas oil millionaires, the Murchison brothers. The first $200,000 went into a 1,200-foot poma lift, ski trails, day lodge, fifty-vehicle parking area, and manager's living quarters.

De Gunzburg kicked off his inaugural season on a sour note. He offended the locals when he suggested the military close Arctic Valley, a competing ski area just north of Anchorage. Only thirty-two skiers showed up for his grand opening, not the hundreds Alyeska expected.

Jim Branch, the area's second manager, arrived just in time to guide the inaugural opening, cope with ten feet of snow in thirty-six hours, and maintain the road system that consisted of a mile of winding, gravel road and homemade bridges.

Branch was a former Dartmouth ski racer and jumper who served in U.S. counterintelligence during World War II. Skiing was his passion and he immediately recognized the area's potential, if not its challenges. So much snow fell that first winter that the road was reduced to a single lane where cars and moose competed for right-of-way.

Wanting to lure more skiers and mend relations with the military, Branch decided to throw a party for the Air Force, complete with a steak dinner. He personally selected the meat and buried it in the snow next to the lodge. On party day, he stepped outside and found that a tracked vehicle had compressed his succulent steaks to the thickness of ham slices, each neatly imprinted with cleat marks.

Money was tight but de Gunzburg pushed forward. In a March 7, 1960, letter to French lift maker Jean Pomagalski, de Gunzburg noted that the poma lift "has been working perfectly and the people of Anchorage are enjoying it immensely. Our crowds are getting larger and larger every weekend." He then ordered Chair 1, a 5,700-foot double chairlift that would rise two thousand vertical feet.

Chair 1 opened Christmas Day under abysmal conditions. Freezing rain turned the area into a skating rink. As early-day skier Eddie Gendzwill recalled, "Cars were sliding down the parking lot hill. Skiers wore garbage sacks over their ski wear to keep from

▲ François de Gunzburg [left] speaks at an Anchorage banquet concluding the 1979 International Airlines Ski Races. With him is Alyeska managing director Chris von Imhof. The enthusiasm and investment of de Gunzburg sparked development of Alyeska in the late 1950s and the 1960s.

▲ A. B. and Frances Clark [Clark Family]

◄◄ François de Gunzburg

[*The Anchorage Times*]

getting wet, hoping to ski in the heavy snow at the higher levels."

Alyeska offered its first season ticket that year at a price of $125 for adults, with a 10 percent discount at participating merchants. But Alaskans weren't used to paying ski lift fees; the lift lines were so short that the chair was known as the millionaires' lift.

De Gunzburg spent much of his time in Alaska in those early years. "He was a friendly, down-to-earth person who dressed in old sweaters, jeans, and

"So François asks to use the phone, calls the French embassy in Washington, yaks in French for fifteen minutes and hands me the receiver. It's the French ambassador, who informs me that Baron de Gunzburg's diplomatic credentials will be at the Air France counter in two hours. From there on we had a little more respect for François."

The financial situation grew worse. De Gunzburg needed more skiers. He went to Washington, D.C., and persuaded national ski authorities to hold the 1963 National Alpine Championships and Olympic trials at his resort. To help land the deal he offered a $130 package for ski competitors that included air travel from Boise, Idaho, to Anchorage and back to Seattle, plus food and lodging in Girdwood. "It was a great boost for the fledgling venture, giving it fame and prominence in ski journals," wrote Atwood.

De Gunzburg opened the slopes to the annual International Airlines Ski Races, sponsored in part by *The Anchorage Times*. He invited America's Olympic sweethearts—downhill racer Penny Pitou

hiking boots," recalled Bob Reeves, an Anchorage attorney who then worked for Matanuska Valley Bank. "He was always in and out of the bank and we'd go out for drinks at five or he'd come over for steaks."

"He was introduced to me as a baron, and I suspected Franny [Frances Clark] was pulling my leg," wrote *Anchorage Times* publisher Atwood. "De Gunzburg looked like a grubby Alaska ski bum in Levis and tank tops."

Reeves discovered just how powerful a French baron could be. De Gunzburg walked into the bank one day, pale and shaken. His mother was very ill and he needed to catch that day's Air France flight to Paris. Air France had no boarding rights in Anchorage and Reeves found out that the only way de Gunzburg could board the plane was as an employee or diplomat.

◄◄ Prince Rupert, Claire Conrad's malamute, takes a ride during the early days of the first chairlift. There were few riders and no lift lines after Chair 1 opened in late 1960. Ten of the lift's 114 seats had wooden backs instead of cold metal ones, and they were in high demand on cold days for the slow ride to the top. [Nancy Simmerman]

◄◄◄ A helicopter and skiers go high up on Mount Alyeska in the late 1950s. François de Gunzburg introduced helicopter service in 1958 to airlift expert skiers to the mountain's upper slopes. Other skiers walked up the slopes or caught a ride on the Girdwood Community Club's weasel before the first lifts went in. Resort promoter Ernie Baumann installed a rope tow in 1956. A poma lift was added in 1959 before the area got its first chairlift, which opened on Christmas Day 1960. [Steve McCutcheon]

◄ This publicity shot of a 1960s-era snow bunny was used to generate interest in the Alyeska ski area. Alyeska's François de Gunzburg commissioned a series of cheesecake shots patterned after a successful Sun Valley promotion. [Alyeska Resort]

Conde Nast Traveler magazine called this view the best at any ski area in North America. This aerial looks over the upper ridge of Alyeska's Glacier Bowl through Glacier Valley and out onto the waters of Turnagain Arm.

and slalom racer Betsy Snite—to tour Alaska to generate enthusiasm for the sport of skiing. And he sold more stock in December 1961 to lease 233 acres at the mountain base for a residential subdivision.

The subdivision grew to eighty residences by the time Jim Branch decided to return with his family to the East Coast. The subdivision provided a reliable skier base for the resort along with a limited cash flow. Branch often bartered the lots for services rendered or offered them in lieu of wages. Son Mike remembers that Branch even paid himself in subdivision lots. It was a continual effort to raise money and keep improving the ski area, but the work was beginning to bear fruit as Alyeska's reputation grew.

The Girdwood 11

Virtually the entire community showed up at an April 9, 1956, special meeting of the Girdwood Community Club to organize a nonprofit organization called the Alyeska Ski Corp. Representatives of eleven families pledged $250 each and the club loaned the new corporation another $500 to purchase 160 acres of land at a June 4 auction.

The Girdwood 11 included Tom Brown, Bob Bursiel, Robert Burns, Joe Danich, Robert Goodwin, Con Hibbs, Joseph Hunt, Edith Lincoln, John Morgestar, Chuck Nicolet, and Wes Traves.

The group was proud of its contribution to the creation of the Alyeska ski area, and when an Anchorage newspaper congratulated that city for the success of the 1963 National Alpine Championships and Olympic trials at Alyeska, they quickly set the record straight.

"By purchasing 160 acres of federal lands on the mountain and pushing a pioneer road into the area, they thereby initiated the first tangible steps in the creation of this major ski area on which the nationals were so recently held," several members of the original eleven wrote in a lengthy letter to *The Anchorage Times.*

"These initial steps were small ones, as the mountain is measured today, but at that time they were almost gigantic—for so small a group, few of whom were skilled on skis, none of whom had ever been remotely connected with the promotion of a ski area.

"Even so, the effort nearly foundered, for when the Girdwood stockholders turned to Anchorage in search of funds to push their development, they met with skepticism, scorn and indifference among many of the Anchorage businessmen, skiers and ski professionals whom they approached. . . . The actual truth was this: Mount Alyeska came into being despite Anchorage, not because of it."

This is Girdwood 1956. The town had little to offer in the way of employment following the bustle of Seward Highway construction that ended in 1951 and before the development of the Alyeska ski area. [CITY OF GIRDWOOD]

43

Virginia Bursiel

▲ Bob Bursiel painted this watercolor of the family's first "home" on Crow Creek. [BURSIEL FAMILY]

▶ Bob and Virginia Bursiel, with their eleven-month-old daughter Genette, pose at their cabin under construction on Crow Creek Road in 1948. When Virginia did the laundry in a nearby stream, she would sing loudly so that Bob would know she was safe from bears. [BURSIEL FAMILY]

Virginia Bursiel calls it the adventure of a lifetime. True pioneers who used a Jeep instead of a plow, Bursiel and her husband, Bob, carved out a comfortable niche well beyond the end of the road, where they raised their eight children.

There were only ten or so folks in Girdwood when the couple arrived in 1948: "two old miners, the couple who owned the lodge and their child, railroad workers, and fireguards."

But the ten stuck together, and with winter on its way that first year, "the folks in Girdwood all came up and hauled our stuff up to this broken-down house with one little intact room, which they fixed up into the kitchen and warm room. They pitched our tent outside the warm room on a big floor."

The first year was hard but satisfying. "It took all your energies just to exist, what with the wood and water to carry, the vegetable garden, meat to shoot, berries to pick and fish to catch."

By November the temperature dived to thirty degrees below zero. Bob was working at Portage, so whenever Virginia needed to use the Jeep she would "take a little cake pan, fill it with rocks, pour in some oil, light it and put it underneath the car to warm it up." With no antifreeze to protect the radiator, she would drain it after each use and refill it with hot water when she was ready to go.

Their first real cabin was sixteen feet by twenty feet, "built by a city boy [Bob] who hadn't built anything like a cabin before." They chinked it with gunnysacks from a nearby gold mine and lived there until their fifth baby was born.

Virginia now lives in a spacious house on Crow Creek Road that Bob built in 1977, filled with Bob's hand-illustrated diaries and their paintings. One daughter lives in the original cabin and most of their other children live nearby. One son drowned in an accident; Bob, Girdwood's longtime mayor, died in 1996.

Looking back on her years at Girdwood, Virginia calls them "the best of all times, living in a beautiful valley, next to a bubbling creek, surrounded by fabulous people."

much as three feet of water at high tide. The Seward Highway was severely damaged, as were all the bridges along the highway and in Glacier Valley.

Most of Girdwood's sixty residents were relocated about two and a half miles up-valley, along with several structures, including Crow Creek Mercantile, the church, and the schoolhouse.

No one was killed or seriously injured in Girdwood. The ski resort suffered little damage, even though an avalanche struck one of the lift towers, but the town lost the popular Little Dipper roadhouse to a chimney fire.

Just five days after the quake, François de Gunzburg wrote Jean Pomagalski, the manufacturer of the ski area's poma lift and chairlift, to tell him, "During the earthquake I saw a 27,000-pound cement counterweight jumping up and down like a matchbox and yet the counterweight tower suffered no damage at all."

The Little Dipper roadhouse burns out of control in the aftermath of the 1964 Good Friday earthquake. Local writer Hugh Cruikshank had just taken a bite of his steak when the building started "swaying back and forth like a ship on a stormy sea" and his meat "went flying across the room." When the shaking slowed, "We finally were able to get out of the building and it started to burn, and it burned to the ground."
[CITY OF GIRDWOOD]

John Trautner

▲ John Trautner

► A "well-dressed" International Airlines Ski Race competitor heads for his race start. John Trautner helped organize the popular race series, which was moved to Alyeska in 1961.

Mornings find him at the Java Haus, where he works on his latest projects and keeps up with the community he loves. His mind is as sharp as ever and his opinions just as passionate. Retirement has not mellowed John Trautner, one of Girdwood's leading civic leaders and philanthropists.

Trautner fought to bring natural gas into the valley, to build a modern sewer system, and to add a lighted bike path to Alyeska Highway after five people, including two brothers and a girl, were struck by cars and died. Thanks to him, many Girdwood children wake up on Christmas morning to find a new bike under their Christmas tree.

Trautner organized the first ski club in Anchorage, the Chugach Ski Club and Racing Association, and held sanctioned races on the area's tiny ski hills. He and Judy Anderson brought off the first International Airlines Ski Races, at Arctic Valley north of Anchorage, to "generate international good will." Eleven airlines participated, and when the master of ceremonies at the awards ceremony fell off the podium after too much to drink, Trautner stepped in and invited the live television audience to come on down for a good time. Soon the Elks Club was packed.

A man of many talents, Trautner set up a first aid station in the back of his station wagon in downtown Anchorage during the 1964 earthquake. "There were people running around in shock, with cuts and bruises. I set and bandaged a broken arm and realized how handy it was to have first aid training." He used those skills to train Girdwood's first emergency medical technicians when he and Joe Danich brought ambulance service to Girdwood in 1970.

Trautner moved to Girdwood in 1969 when he was hired as director of administration for the ski resort. It was a short-lived job, and he went on to work with Bruce Ficke at the resort's condominium development. He acquired Joe Danich's service station in the mid-1970s, added a retail mall, and sold it all to Tesoro Alaska Company in 1996. In the interim, he picked up a couple of college degrees and several gold claims on Canyon Creek, where he has worked every summer since 1982.

Georgia and Dallas Pitzer

Skiing was over for the day, the lifts had closed, and Georgia Pitzer had just sat down in the day lodge when she experienced the shaking of her life.

"The building started rocking and rolling so violently you could see daylight out the sides. Locke Jacobs, Harvey Johnson, and I headed out the door on the mountainside but the wind was roaring at avalanche speed and totally encased us in snow. We couldn't open the door to get back in so Locke pushed the glass out.

"Inside everything was in turmoil, bricks flying off the fireplace. We just stood frozen for what seemed like an eternity," but was only the longest four minutes of her life. When the 1964 Good Friday earthquake finally ended, resort manager Jim Branch warned everyone to get out fast before an avalanche could strike.

"We lived in a company house just below where the first condos went in," Pitzer said. "I ran in and grabbed my beaver coat and Chantilly perfume. Fortunately Dallas [her husband] had the presence to grab sleeping bags, food, and pots and pans."

The Pitzers owned a little ten-foot-by-twenty-foot cabin down the road that became home for the next eight days for them and fifteen others, including Alyeska's avalanche expert Don Flynn, his wife, Hilda, and their baby. They melted snow for water and for washing the diapers, which they hung up to dry on a piece of string. "We learned to do a lot with a little," Georgia said. Gary King flew in to check on their safety and to pick up postcards to let the rest of the world know they were safe. Georgia wrote hers with an eyebrow pencil, the only writing instrument she could find.

The Pitzers came to Alaska in 1947 looking for jobs. After stints in the Fairbanks region, where they worked on what became Fort Wainwright and Eielson Air Force Base, they moved to Indian, about fifteen miles north of Girdwood. Dallas operated a school bus and also worked at the Alyeska Ski Resort, clearing trees and helping to build Chair 1.

That was the beginning of a long relationship between the resort and the Pitzers. Dallas went on to become mountain manager, lift foreman, and heavy equipment operator, while Georgia worked for ten years in the snack bar and twenty-eight years as ticket office manager.

Georgia Pitzer tallies up the day's sales as Sam Rapphahn straightens up. Georgia retired to Indian, about ten miles north of Girdwood, while Sam moved to Washington, D.C., with the U.S. Fish and Wildlife Service. [DAVID PREDEGER]

51

The Double Musky

The lights of the Double Musky illuminate the snow around the restaurant in this photo from 1983. Julian and Kay Maule opened the Double Musky in 1962 and drew crowds for drinks, dinner, and polka music. The restaurant is widely known now for its Cajun cuisine.

It started with a simple invitation. Jerry Bernas met up with Julian Maule one day, and Maule invited Bernas down to his cabin for a musky: muscatel wine and ginger ale.

Soon the whole group known as the Millionaire's Club—so called because there were so few skiers on the mountain that they virtually had the chairlift to themselves—began gathering at Julian and Kay's cabin on Crow Creek Road. Julian would say, "Have a musky, c'mon have a double musky," and Kay would cook up a batch of spaghetti.

Eventually club members suggested the Maules build a bar and restaurant, but when it was time to open for business in 1962, they couldn't agree on a name. They considered Crow Creek Lodge, Alyeska Lodge, Big Bear Bar, Moose Juice Joint. Finally Bernas announced that the only appropriate name was the Double Musky.

The Double Musky Inn quickly became the hot spot with good food and good entertainment. As Loverne Bercee recalls: "Kay would cook steaks on the open fireplace grill, Julian would pour drinks at the bar." After dinner, they would push back the picnic tables and dance.

"Polka Dan [Zantek] put his heart and soul into his rendition of the polka, waltzes, and romantic Russian ballads. Hermann the German [Hastreiter] would come in on the zither.

"Carl Lind and Danny Bome would accompany Polka Dan on washtub bass. Carl would take a couple of spoons from the table and begin rapping them in a kind of staccato tempo to keep time with the music.

"The Two Loose Moose—George McCoy and John Trautner—would join in, with George on his accordion and John in perfect time on the garbage can bass. Sometimes John would reach in his pocket and grab his mouth organ."

Bob and Deanna Persons bought the Double Musky in 1979, changed its menu to classic New Orleans Cajun dishes prepared with Alaska seafood, and expanded it into what *Esquire Magazine* called "the last great American roadhouse."

Loverne Bercee

For a woman who was scared of mountains when she arrived, Loverne Bercee found peace, if not prosperity, on Alyeska's slopes.

She learned to conquer the mountain and to use it to help make a living. She opened Alyeska's first retail shop and later became the mountain's historian, authoring Girdwood's most encompassing book, *True Tales from the Top of Mt. Alyeska.* A petite blonde with a gentle, inquiring nature, she evolved into the spiritual soul of the resort, the one who captures the area's essence in poetry, song, and stories.

A native of Edmonton, Canada, Loverne drove to Anchorage in 1957 and found herself a stranger in a strange land. She was a city girl in a backwoods place, desperately homesick as she worked a variety of jobs and tried to fit in.

Her introduction to Alyeska came in 1967. Her sixteen-year-old sister had driven to Alaska in a 1952 Chevy and wanted to learn to ski. The two piled into the old car with bald tires and made it to within ten miles of Alyeska when they lost control and found themselves pointed back toward Anchorage. Fortunately mountain ranger Chuck O'Leary was behind them and delivered them safely to the resort.

They spent the day with Gary King, head of the ski school, who invited the attractive sisters to the Double Musky for dinner and drinks.

Loverne fell in love with Girdwood and its mountain—and with Jerry Bernas. They were married and lived in a house in Girdwood that they built together. After her marriage ended, she wed Girdwood painter Mirco Bercee.

Today she arranges flowers at the Alyeska Prince Hotel and writes for the local newspaper.

▲ Loverne Bercee

Connie Hibbs

When Connie Hibbs was eight years old, her mom loaded a homemade motor home and drove to Alaska. Ten family members made the two-week trip from Spokane, Washington, in 1951."

"It was my mom's dream come true, not my dad's," Connie says. "He always called himself a real sourdough—sour on the country, but didn't have enough dough to get out."

The ten family members got as far as Girdwood, where four of them ended up working for the railroad. Mother Dorothy applied for unemployment benefits when her job ended, but she was turned down because the position of Girdwood postmaster had just opened up. Dorothy said she didn't know how to be a postmaster but was told she had to take the job anyway. She accepted the job, keeping it until she retired in 1977 when her daughter, Connie, took over the position.

There were twenty families in the area when the Hibbs family arrived. "It was an unbelievable place to be a kid," Connie says. "There were so many old cabins that when we played house, everyone had their own."

It took eight students for a school to qualify for having a schoolteacher, and that first year the community was short one child. "The Williams family had just arrived, so their oldest son, who was really smart, had to take the eighth grade over again so we could get our teacher."

▲ The ten members of the Hibbs family arrived in a homemade motor home in 1951. Pictured here [from left] are cousin Karen Sikes and Hibbs children Connie, Janie, Pat, Jack, and Judy.

[HIBBS FAMILY]

53

3

The
Flight
Deck

By 1967 the French baron, François de Gunzburg, had little time for a ski resort that always needed more work and more investment. He was now focused on his growing business interests in Europe and his widespread activities that included a seat on the Alaska Airlines board of directors. When the airline offered a stock swap for the ski resort, de Gunzburg said yes, ushering in one of the most colorful eras in Alyeska's history.

Charlie Willis, the airline's flamboyant president, promised the sky: "First-class hotel, heated swimming pool, additional ski lifts, ice skating and curling rink, golf range, bridle paths and an international advertising and sales program," according to the inaugural press release announcing the airline's plans for the resort.

But Alaska Airlines didn't have the money to finance these improvements. The company had its own cash woes and told the resort's new general manager, Chris von Imhof, that he was basically on his own.

Von Imhof managed to deliver on most of Willis's

commitments. He found Bruce Ficke, who figured out how to finance a hotel and related condominium development. And he used creative financing to build three new chairlifts, including one bankrolled by donations and the hard work of Bud Gibbs.

Von Imhof worked with his mountain manager, Don Conrad, and senior ski patrolman Eddie Gendzwill to improve avalanche control, while expanding the ski racing program and introducing fun events like spring carnival to provide a steady clientele.

Alyeska and von Imhof shared center stage with Rick Mystrom in two bids to host the Winter Olympics and surprised the world by hosting a successful world-cup ski race and the annual International Airlines Ski Races, sponsored in part by Bob Atwood's *Anchorage Times.*

The small town of Girdwood grew, too, incorporating itself as a first-class city with Bob Bursiel as its longtime mayor and opening its doors during the annual Forest Fair, where Nina von Imhof's dancers were the hit of center stage.

A gutsy competitor makes a rousing, full-bore leap into a pool of water during the 1979 Slush Cup fun at Alyeska. The idea is to sail into the water, then ski [or snowboard] across the pool. Racers are judged on costume creativity, air gained, hang time, style, distance, and crowd enthusiasm. It's all part of Alyeska's annual spring carnival.

Chris
von Imhof

Mr. Alyeska

His vision always seems to outstrip his resources, but his infectious enthusiasm makes remarkable things happen. Chris von Imhof has turned a modest ski area with a single lift into a four-season resort that's ready to become a vacation destination for the world.

"Chris just doesn't give up," says longtime friend Bob Reeves. "Things fall down, things break, there's no money in the bank, Chris just keeps on going until he figures a way out."

Von Imhof thrives on challenge and adversity. "So undercapitalized, so underfinanced, that I almost got laughed out of the bank just trying to buy a snow cat," von Imhof recalls of the early years at Alyeska. "There were times when I had to scrape together the payroll, and I would tell my folks they better hustle to the bank."

Yet without much help from his bosses at Alaska Airlines, he managed to build a hotel, expand restaurant services, construct three new chairlifts, introduce snowmaking and night lighting, and improve avalanche control.

This was the Alaska Airlines era—1967–1980—a period that began as flamboyantly as the airline's larger-than-life president, Charlie Willis. In the June 21, 1967, press release announcing the airline's lease-purchase agreement and management contract for Alyeska, Willis promised to construct "a large new hotel that features dining facilities done in Alaskana decor and a chalet-type bar and grille, spacious lobby facilities, a sauna and rathskeller," along with new chairlifts and vastly expanded recreational facilities.

The agreement included von Imhof as Alyeska's new vice president and general manager.

"I was proud to join at a time of great progress," von Imhof said, "but when I went to Seattle for my first meeting, I discovered there was no money to back up the plans." The struggling airline could barely pay its own bills, much less front the $1 million in first-year construction costs. Besides, it was prohibited from investing in hotels and subsidiaries because of terms of a federal aviation subsidy it received.

Willis informed von Imhof that it was up to him to build the hotel. Von Imhof's response: "This indeed was going to be a challenge."

A year later, von Imhof found another man who believed that the resort had a great future: Bruce Ficke, an Anchorage insurance agency owner. The resort entered into a lease-purchase agreement with Ficke for a thirty-two-unit hotel, dining room, cocktail lounge, and convention facilities, with a second phase that included more units, heated outdoor swimming pool, and ice-skating rink.

Ficke delivered phase one and the grand opening was memorable. Von Imhof invited everyone who was anyone out to the resort for a great party. A huge storm roared in and knocked out the power, leaving the hotel with no lights and no water.

"The governor was here, Charlie Willis was here, and we couldn't flush the toilets or turn on the lights," von Imhof recalls. "So we lit a bunch of candles and served the scotch straight."

Von Imhof calls those early years a time of peaks and valleys—with few peaks and many valleys, such as the April afternoon in 1969 when Per Bjorn-Roli and a group of other skiers were sipping beer and listening to Polka Dan at the day lodge after a great day on the slopes.

"We heard a rumble and looked out and saw the canyon full of debris and timbers," Bjorn-Roli said. "It's moving so slow you could walk next to it, like a lava flow. But it keeps coming and coming, growing bigger and bigger. It swallows two snow machines and takes out the lift shack and heads straight for the day lodge.

"That's when all of us bail out except my buddy Wally Kinnunen. He sat there at the window, finishing his beer while the avalanche rolled to a stop just ten feet away." In one of life's ironies, the avalanche had been inadvertently set off by mountain ranger Chuck O'Leary.

The next morning von Imhof called in the ski

▲ Chris and Nina von Imhof

◄ When Alaska Airlines took over Alyeska in 1967, new general manager Chris von Imhof quickly found "that Alaska Airlines had even less money than the Alyeska Ski Corporation." To reduce expenses, he and his wife, Nina, provided the "talent" for the airline's first two brochures. [ALYESKA RESORT]

◄◄ Chris von Imhof [FRANK FLAVIN]

The air traffic control tower at Anchorage International Airport lies in ruins following the 1964 earthquake. Chris von Imhof was at work at the airport when the trembler hit. He rescued two people caught in the tower rubble, then returned to his devastated office to retrieve the cash box and company records. [ANCHORAGE MUSEUM OF HISTORY AND ART]

report: "Good morning, skiers. I have some good news and bad news. There's twenty-five feet of snow at base, but our one and only chairlift was hit by an avalanche so I hereby declare the season closed."

Von Imhof later expanded the ski resort to the point that it needed a second chairlift, and he arranged financing through the manufacturer, using real estate as collateral. "It was a difficult project but we researched it well, drawing from twenty years of snow data from the Forest Service to lay it out. We wanted to be well away from an avalanche zone."

Chair 2 opened in 1972, giving skiers more terrain with reliably good snow conditions and bringing von Imhof his first profitable season. As thanks, Alaska Airlines named the lift after him.

Then disaster struck on April 14, 1973, the fifth day of a resort closure due to heavy storms. The mountain crew had been shooting virtually nonstop at slide-prone areas with 75 mm artillery to set off avalanches and clear dangerous slopes. Von Imhof got an early-morning call to come look in the canyon.

There he found the base terminal and two of the Chair 2 towers, victims of a huge natural avalanche.

Insurance covered all but ten thousand dollars of the loss. Chair 2 was moved farther up the mountain, and von Imhof went looking for bigger artillery: the 75 mm guns were no match for a serious avalanche mountain. With help from Ted Stevens, Alaska's senior U.S. senator, Alyeska became one of the first ski resorts to obtain 105 mm guns from the military.

The Alaska Airlines era was one of personal challenge for von Imhof, who almost lost his oldest son in a house fire, almost lost his own life in a helicopter crash, and arrived home one night to find his family held hostage by robbers waiting for the keys to the resort's safe. They took sixty thousand dollars, the entire proceeds from that year's spring carnival, but they were later caught and convicted.

Like his predecessors James Girdwood and François de Gunzburg, von Imhof is a consummate optimist who is handsome, ebullient, and everyone's friend. "He's truly one of the most likeable guys you could ever meet, with that great smile and remarkable ability to remember everyone's name," says Larry Daniels, his longtime resort manager. "People love him. So many that we call them FOCs—friends of Chris."

He was born in Berlin, of aristocratic blood, one of three sons in a family that once ruled Nuremberg. When his father died on the Russian front during World War II, his mother moved the family to the resort town of Garmisch-Partenkirchen, where his father's uncle ran the best hotel in town. He apprenticed with his great-uncle, attended hotel management school, and then moved to Paris, as was the tradition with those who wanted to get ahead in the business.

He spent six months in France before he met an American family who would sponsor his immigration to America. "Americans always impressed me with their entrepreneurial attitude," he said. "I wanted to go to the land of great opportunity."

Von Imhof left Naples, Italy, in 1959 on a ship bound for New York City. He drove to Los Angeles, where he started out as a front-desk agent on the night shift for the Beverly Hilton Hotel, the most luxurious hotel in town. He enrolled part-time at Santa Monica Community College and later at UCLA.

After six months of active duty in the Marine Corps, he decided to try something different and became the Anchorage sales and operational manager for SAS Scandinavian Airlines. SAS used Anchorage as a stopover on its polar flights from Europe to Asia. He arrived in 1963 in the dark of winter, an inauspicious introduction to Alaska that quickly warmed with ski treks to Alyeska and the company of willing young flight attendants.

When the job of state director of tourism became vacant, Von Imhof applied. *Anchorage Times* publisher Bob Atwood lobbied for him—von Imhof was dating the publisher's daughter at the time—as did bank executive Bob Reeves. Atwood sponsored his application for citizenship, a requirement for state employment.

"I first met Governor Bill Egan at the mansion for lunch," von Imhof recalled. "It was a nice, casual affair, so different from European tradition. The governor asked me if I had any skeletons in my closet. I didn't understand that vernacular phrase so replied, 'No, I haven't shot anyone.'"

Von Imhof got the job and spent two years in the state capital, Juneau. Then political regimes changed and Wally Hickel took over as governor. Von Imhof knew the end was near when a long-overdue brochure produced by his office featured the former governor's picture.

"I got such a big lecture from Governor Wally Hickel that I ended the conversation with 'Heil Hickel.'" It was time for von Imhof to move on.

Von Imhof had talked with Alaska Airlines about the state's lack of a winter program and the airline's president, Charlie Willis "understood the potential of this little ski area. He asked me to be part of the future," von Imhof said.

As Alyeska grew, von Imhof became a larger part of that future than perhaps either he or Willis could have imagined.

The friendly glow of night lighting, introduced in 1980, lengthens the skiing day at Alyeska. One skier told *The Anchorage Times* that the lights "look like a 6,000-foot-long Christmas tree. You can sometimes see it halfway to Anchorage on the highway." Lights now illuminate more than two thousand vertical feet of terrain, including twenty-seven trails.

Alaska Airlines

The roots of Alaska Airlines were humble: a three-passenger Stinson with MCGEE AIRLINES painted on the side. It was an all-charter operation in the early 1930s, with pilots responsible for filling their planes with passengers and freight.

McGee merged with several other small carriers and ended the decade as the largest airline in the territory. It changed its name with frequency—McGee Airways, Star Air Service, Star Air Lines, Alaska Star Airlines—finally settling on Alaska Airlines in 1944.

The company's operations remained strictly Alaskan until 1951 when the Civil Aeronautics Authority awarded it the right to fly from Anchorage and Fairbanks to Seattle and Portland. The new route changed the airline forever.

By 2003, Alaska Airlines ranked as the nation's ninth largest airline, with a modern fleet of jets flying up and down the West Coast and across the nation.

During the reign of Charlie Willis as president, from 1957 to 1972, Alaska Airlines ventured far from its core business. It purchased Bell Island, a fishing resort near Ketchikan, which needed a lot of fixing up, along with the Potlatch House in Sitka and the Wickersham House in Juneau. It signed a three-year management agreement with Alyeska Ski Corp. in 1967 to operate the resort, and later purchased it outright.

The airline got into the newspaper business after the Nome paper published something Willis didn't like. He bought the paper and installed publishing legend Albro Gregory as its editor. Willis had similar disagreements with publishers in Petersburg and Wrangell, and the airline ended up with a chain of small newspapers

When the airline's board removed Willis as president in 1972, the new leadership sold off its non-airline subsidiaries.

Nina von Imhof is the musher as Alaska Governor Keith Miller prepares for a dogsled ride during the opening of Alyeska's Nugget Inn in 1969. Looking on are Chris von Imhof, at left, and Alaska Airlines President Charlie Willis. [ALASKA AIRLINES]

Charlie Willis

Confidant to presidents, one of the most decorated airmen in World War II, promoter extraordinaire, Charlie Willis had few peers.

When he took over Alaska Airlines in 1957, the company was in shambles and the paperwork to revoke its certificate sat on President Dwight Eisenhower's desk. (A presidential signature was required to revoke the certificate of an international carrier, and Alaska Airlines was considered an international carrier because it flew to Whitehorse, Canada.)

"Charlie went in to see Ike—he had been his chief of staff—and told him he could probably buy the airline's certificate if the president didn't sign off on its revocation," recalled Bob Reeves, a Willis friend and a former member of the airline's board. "So Ike said, 'Here's your certificate,'" and Willis became the new owner.

Willis was fun and unpredictable. For the inaugural flight of DC-6 service, he installed a piano and stand-up bar in the front of the plane. Willis tended bar while his wife, composer-musician Elizabeth Firestone Willis, banged out tunes on the piano.

He introduced Gold Nugget and Golden Samovar service, complete with crimson- and velvet-clad flight attendants and cabins, and turned his office into a saloon with swinging doors, player piano, and beer on tap. He drew up the letter of intent to purchase the carrier's first Boeing aircraft on the back of a negotiating attorney's shirt.

"He was a fascinating guy who had about a hundred ideas a day," Reeves said. "You had to be careful because one or two of them would be great."

He introduced in-flight movies, seats that could be folded into tables, speakers so passengers could listen to music, and food so good that a rival carrier filed a complaint with the Civil Aeronautics Board, charging that Alaska served luxury meals in coach. Actually, Alaska bought meals from Sally's Box Lunch in Fairbanks while Pan American's meals were catered by Maxim's of Paris.

"He really built the airline and he did it on a shoestring," Reeves said. "People thought Charlie had a lot of money because he was married to Elizabeth Firestone but the Firestones had a prenuptial agreement so tight he couldn't borrow a dime."

Financial problems ended Willis's aviation career in 1972 when the board of directors, except for Reeves, voted to remove him from office.

Charlie Willis poses in his frontier office at Alaska Airlines in this photo from the 1960s. The Alaska Airlines president rescued a failing airline and introduced innovations now considered commonplace. Willis also understood how properties such as Alyeska could generate needed winter business. [ALASKA AIRLINES]

The Nugget Inn

Resort to the lavish life" read the first advertisements for Alyeska's new Nugget Inn.

A bit of an overstatement perhaps, but the grand opening of this rustic, chalet-type hotel played a critical role in the economic future of the resort. Alyeska now had good overnight accommodations so the ski area could handle full charter tours from the Lower 48 states.

The thirty-two-room hotel with cocktail lounge and restaurant opened February 1, 1969, just in time to provide housing for the 1969 Junior National Alpine and Nordic Ski Championships.

Bruce Ficke and Associates of Anchorage built the inn under a lease-purchase agreement with Alaska Airlines. Its second phase included a wing containing forty condominium units sold to the public but rented out by the hotel when not in use, and an outdoor heated swimming pool.

The Nugget's interior featured Alaska gold rush decor to match the interiors of Alaska Airlines planes. "What I wanted was the interior of a whore-house," Charlie Willis, Alaska's colorful president, once explained.

The airline heavily promoted the inn and provided transportation for its first guests, a tour group of forty-five from Seattle who paid only $250 for room and lift tickets for one week and round-trip air travel between Seattle and Anchorage.

The opening of the thirty-two-room Nugget Inn in 1969, and its associated condominium development, gave Alyeska the basic hospitality infrastructure it needed to market itself beyond Anchorage. Alaska Airlines promoted the rustic hotel as "truly deluxe by any standard." [ALASKA AIRLINES]

Bruce Ficke

He was a true believer in Alyeska's future, a man who figured out how to finance a venture no other investor would touch.

Bruce Ficke stepped in and built the thirty-two-room Nugget Inn and three condominium projects that gave the resort the property base it needed to mature into profitability. He did it with ingenuity, introducing an ownership option that allowed middle-class skiers to buy in, while providing the resort with additional bedrooms when the condo owners were not on site.

An Air Force veteran who established a successful insurance business in Anchorage, Ficke's first venture in Girdwood was a hayride. "We had such a good time, and you could see that [nearby] Anchorage needed its own resort."

Ficke decided to build a hotel at Girdwood, plus condominiums—the first ever constructed in Alaska. He needed a bank to handle the mortgage on the hotel. Matanuska Valley Bank was interested but didn't have enough reserves until Ficke, along with some family and friends, moved their accounts into the bank.

He worked with attorney Charlie Tulin on state legislation that allowed condominium ownership. "We were in such a huge hurry to get the act passed that Charlie's wife would type, type, type into the night," Ficke said. The bill passed in a matter of weeks. "It was a lot easier to do business in those days."

Ever the cautious insurance man, Ficke insisted on installing sprinkler systems in the wood structures he built. That required a reliable water source—"the Girdwood utilities would go out three times a day"—so he built a large outdoor swimming pool in front of his first condo project. He also ended up installing his own power system.

The condos sold well. "I had a great bunch of buyers—a supreme court justice, the chair of Wien Air Alaska, the publisher of the *Anchorage Daily News*."

Ficke tried to buy the Alyeska resort from Alaska Airlines but the deal fell through and the airline bought Ficke out instead, giving him stock for his interest in the hotel. Ficke moved to Hawaii, where he has remained active in the business community.

▲ **Bruce Ficke** [Bob Spring]

◀ Famous for its sourdough bread and sweet-rolls, the Bake Shop is a favorite spot for Girdwood visitors and residents. Former Alyeska chef Werner Egloff opened the eatery in 1972 in a ground-level condominium built by Bruce Ficke.

Skiers of the Future

One of the world's best youth ski programs is located on the slopes of Mount Alyeska. Founded in 1962, the Alyeska Ski Club and Snowboard Club offers programs that range from entry-level ski racing and boarding to training for elite-level athletes.

Longtime Girdwood resident Don Conrad started Alyeska's Mighty Mites, the beginning program for kids as young as six, in the early 1960s. "This program was so successful because it was so simple," said Bud Gibbs, a longtime Mighty Mites coach. "We didn't have a bunch of rules and weren't involved with any national associations. We just

came down every Sunday and skied with the kids. Charged them ten dollars and gave them a five-dollar hat. When we needed things . . . the parents would take up a collection.

"We taught them citizenship, a healthy lifestyle, and helped them use up a lot of energy. The Mighty Mite kids I coached are the coaches of today, like a renewable resource."

Larry Daniels, general manager for the Alyeska ski area, credits the racing program for much of the resort's success: "Alyeska Ski Club is . . . the foundation of our most dedicated customers and provides a lot of support when we host big events."

Gibbs said there were days in the early years when the racers' parents were the only customers at the Nugget Inn. "The bar manager used to complain that the kids messed up his bar until I reminded him that if we didn't have these kids, he wouldn't have any parents to drink in his bar."

The club trains about two hundred young people each year, employing a full-time program director and thirty coaches.

Young Mighty Mite racers test their skills. The Mighty Mite program began in the early 1960s and quickly grew into one of the premier ski education programs in the nation thanks to its simple rules, skilled coaches, and dedicated volunteers. [Alyeska Resort]

Bud Gibbs

Some call him the old man of the mountain, but Bud Gibbs out-skis most people one-third his age.

"He goes like a son-of-a-gun, hard to shake at 60-65 miles per hour," said fellow racer Per Bjorn-Roli. "He's a skiing miracle, back on the mountain in January after getting two new knees in November."

Gibbs put his new knees to the ultimate test five months after the operation when he took a major spill that cracked his helmet, tore much of the skin from his face, and left him with a mild concussion. He was back on the mountain within days—with a new helmet, his sole acknowledgement of his advancing age.

An amiable Texan who first came to Alaska in 1951 to fish commercially, Gibbs credits skiing with keeping him young. "I can always rely on that mountain and gravity. Skiing keeps me in top physical shape and that keeps me from getting old."

He's a national downhill champion who won the 2001 Masters competition by four seconds on a forty-seven-second course.

Gibbs has skied Alyeska since it first opened in 1959 and, while he cuts a fast figure on the mountain, he has been a major figure in creation of one of the nation's most successful youth training programs. He coached in the Mighty Mites program for eighteen years, instilling core values of citizenship and respect along with ski instruction.

He dedicated two years to construction of the Tanaka chairlift, which services the race training hill, putting in four weeks of vacation plus weekends. At one point, he recalls, "I took my whole family, including my daughters, down to Alyeska and they poured concrete like troopers."

He managed to cover $150,000 of the $175,000 project cost through donated labor and material.

Gibbs raised three outstanding racers: daughter Tracey, who was the first University of Alaska Anchorage female skier to make All-American, daughter Cindy, and son Grant.

"I've lived a golden era here," says Gibbs. He retired in 1998, then built a bed and breakfast and opened up an ice cream shop with his wife, the former Carol Makar, herself the mother of two remarkable racers, Mike and Tony Makar, who learned to ski on Mount Alyeska.

▲ Bud Gibbs

▶ The Gibbses: Tracey, Grant, and Cindy [Gibbs Family]

Rick Mystrom

Rick Mystrom

He's the consummate visionary with the ability to rally folks around what many would call an impossible dream.

Like hosting the Winter Olympics. Rick Mystrom convinced a community mired in economic depression that they could host the world.

"He brought Anchorage together, created a real pride in the community and a can-do spirit that we could be whatever we wanted to be," said longtime Olympic supporter Chris von Imhof, Alyeska's vice president and managing director.

Big ideas come naturally to this man who arrived in Anchorage in 1972 with a head full of dreams, a family, and no means of support. He got a job selling advertising and then formed one of Alaska's most successful advertising agencies. He became increasingly involved in the community, founding Big Brothers/Big Sisters of Anchorage and the Rotarians Sharing program.

His passion was sports. He coached more than twenty youth sports teams and co-chaired the 1992 Great Alaska High School Basketball Classic. So it surprised no one when he decided to put together a citizens group to pursue bringing the Olympics to Anchorage.

"It all happened over a luncheon at the Corsair Restaurant," von Imhof recalled. "We discussed the possibility of our local area putting in an Olympic bid. We certainly had all the necessary ingredients, along with excellent worldwide accessibility, to present a very successful program."

Mystrom led the group in the successful effort to be the U.S. Olympic Committee's choice for the 1992 and 1994 Olympic winter games. These games were eventually held in other countries and Anchorage lost out to Salt Lake City for the 2002 games.

Mystrom went on to a political career as an Anchorage Assembly member and two-term mayor of the city. Today he develops real estate, including a golf course in Washington state.

1992 Winter Olympics

Anchorage and the Olympics

Anchorage's Olympic dreams sprang from the ashes of the 1964 earthquake and the vision of Sewell "Stumpy" Faulkner, then an Anchorage city councilman, consummate skier, and real estate man.

"The Winter Olympic Committee is all ready for Council approval Monday night," he wrote in his diary on October 11, 1964. "Our chances may be many years away but there is no harm in starting now."

Faulkner was right in his assessment of Anchorage's chances of snaring the Winter Olympics. But that didn't stop Alyeska's Chris von Imhof, who went to Chicago in 1966 with businessman Jack Anderson and Anchorage Mayor George Byer to make a pitch before the International Olympic Committee. The committee rejected Anchorage's bid due to the community's small population and a housing shortage.

"This was a premature bid," von Imhof said, "but at least we gained an insight into how we should go about it the next time."

Von Imhof attended the 1984 competition in Sarajevo, and "I realized Alaska was just as able to host a fine winter Olympic event." So did Rick Mystrom, an advertising man with big dreams and political aspirations. The pitch for the 1992 Olympics positioned Anchorage as being in the right place at the right time, and Alyeska as the perfect venue for all the alpine competition.

"Anchorage is a young, vibrant, international city selected three times as one of America's outstanding cities," Mystrom wrote. "A city accessible to the world, in a beautiful setting; a city filled with energy, excited by the challenge, united by the Olympic spirit, committed to Olympic ideals, and prepared to welcome the world with open hearts and open homes in 1992."

Anchorage lost its first bid to Albertville, France,

hometown of skiing legend Jean Claude Killey. The loss of the formal bid, made in 1986, was not unexpected, as few cities win the nod the first time around.

The bid for the 1994 Olympics, which Anchorage made in 1988, emphasized the community's strategic location. Equidistant between Asia and Europe, Anchorage's time zone would enable more people to view the games live. Anchorage came tantalizingly close but Lillehammer, Norway, emerged the victor, and the U.S. Olympic Committee chose Salt Lake City for the 2002 games.

Skiers stage an "Olympic" moment at the top of Alyeska as part of the community's bid to host the winter Olympics. The U.S. Olympics Committee selected Anchorage as its choice for the 1992 and 1994 games. While Alaska lost both bids, two of its skiers won downhill gold and silver in the games.

Eddie Gendzwill

▲ **Eddie Gendzwill** [GENDZWILL ESTATE]

▶ Fiddlehead ferns cover the lower slopes of Max's Mountain, unofficially named for Olympic skier Max Marolt. The daredevil skier bet he could beat a helicopter, piloted by Link Luckett, down from the top of the unnamed mountain. There was thirteen feet of snow in 1960; Marolt had a straight shot down, and beat the helicopter by a mile. Marolt died on his skis in 2003 while skiing in the Andes. The official name for the prominence is Baumann's Peak, in recognition of Ernie Baumann, who was instrumental in Alyeska's beginnings.

Eddie Gendzwill carved a fine line on the ski slope, on the dance floor, and with his exquisite carpentry. The son of a count who fled to the United States after political upheaval in Poland, he was one of the earliest skiers on Mount Alyeska.

"At first we had to hike up the mountain; then, as popularity increased, Super Cubs [airplanes] and helicopters started hauling the skiers up. They would land us on Max's Mountain. With the terrain of 'mashed potatoes,' it was more an adventure than a ski run."

Like so many other early skiers, Gendzwill came to Alaska with the military, assigned to Elmendorf Air Force Base during World War II. He took up skiing in 1953 and moved to Girdwood in 1958, where he built a log cabin and got a job at the resort constructing the bar and ticket office. He earned a reputation as a top craftsman and was hired to refurbish the mountaintop Roundhouse and build the beautiful Skyride Restaurant. He also built Locke Jacobs' signature cabin at the resort's base.

Gendzwill was a popular figure on Saturday nights at the Double Musky Inn, where women would line up to dance with him. And he was known throughout the valley for his glacier cocktails, made from a secret, and highly potent, recipe.

Gendzwill was a slim, gentle man, empathetic but a perfectionist. "Everyone loved him," Loverne Bercee said. When it was time to elect a new mayor in 1969, the community drafted Gendzwill, who served a single year before "politics did me in."

Nina von Imhof

She was vivacious, talented, and sometimes larger than life. Nina von Imhof filled Girdwood with laughter, beauty, and dance.

Her laugh was infectious and her personality mischievous. She and a friend once streaked the barroom at the Double Musky, and she thought nothing of mushing the wilderness in search of adventure.

"I had the most amazing mom in the world," wrote eldest son Rudi. "How many moms had bagged a huge polar bear in the arctic or could handle a dog team like a professional musher during the day, then step onto the stage in the evening with so much grace, poise, and talent that she took your breath away?"

She liked a good time, but she most loved her family, her flowers, and her dance. She somehow balanced the needs of three active boys and husband Chris von Imhof with her desire to teach dance to hundreds of Girdwood children and nurture the most beautiful flowers in town.

Born in Nome, she grew up at her family's gold mine, the Rainbow, where she bossed her two brothers and played in a pile of mastodon bones. Dad Frank Whaley was a bush pilot; mom Neva was a champion swimmer and diver and member of the U.S. Olympic team.

She graduated from Fairbanks High School in 1961 and was crowned Miss Alaska in 1963. Wien Air Alaska had a tradition of hiring the woman who was named Miss Alaska, so she went to work for what was then Alaska's largest in-state carrier.

Somewhere along the way she spotted Chris and wanted an introduction, which came during an airlines industry meeting at the Olympic Hotel in Seattle. They married September 30, 1967, at Holy Family Cathedral in Anchorage and moved to Girdwood, where Chris had been named manager of the Alyeska ski resort. Except for a ten-year break when Chris worked on hotel development in Hawaii, Girdwood was Nina's home. Nina died of cancer in 2002 at the age of fifty-eight.

To Chris, she was always "my bride, as beautiful on the inside as the outside," but to Girdwood residents she was Miss Nina, proprietress of Nina's Danceworks, or Miss Nina, the flower queen. Nina's flower beds spread well beyond her yard when she decided to beautify all of Girdwood and create what's now called the Great Wall of Nina, a hillside of perennials along the pathway that connects the Prince Hotel with the rest of Girdwood. Dozens of friends turned out in 2003 to greatly expand Nina's plantings and install a fountain as a tribute to an icon of beauty.

▲ Dancers trained by Nina von Imhof put on a 1983 show at the Girdwood Forest Fair. For years, the von Imhof dancers were the most popular entertainment at the annual fair. She handmade all the colorful costumes.

◄ Nina von Imhof introduces croquet on the green, in August 1982, an event that has everyone dressed in Girdwood's version of formal British attire. Nina loved a good time, almost as much as she loved her family, her dance, and her flowers. [KEN GRAHAM]

Bob Atwood

He left his imprint throughout the state, lobbying long and hard for the military, statehood, and a diversified economy that included a four-season resort in Girdwood. Bob Atwood understood that the visitor industry would become an anchor of Alaska's economy, and he used his newspaper, *The Anchorage Times,* to champion resort development.

Atwood built one of the first chalets at the base of the resort. "Bob wanted to promote Alyeska so he built a nice big house. He didn't ski very much but he enjoyed Girdwood and would sit and read all weekend," said Bob Reeves, an old family friend.

While his chalet stood as a sentinel of his personal belief in the area, he used his newspaper to sell Alyeska to the world. Times were tough for the little resort, which was severely undercapitalized and had too few skiers to pay the bills.

"Several of us agreed that something must be done to stave off bankruptcy for the first major recreational investment in Alaska such as the community had dreamed of and now had at its doorstep," Atwood wrote in one of his newspaper columns. "Our ad hoc group came up with a plan that we hoped would bring international fame and glory—and consequently international skiers—to Alyeska."

The plan was to have Alyeska as the venue for the annual International Airlines Ski Races, open to every air carrier in the world. *The Anchorage Times* sponsored the races, giving them liberal news coverage and editorial support.

"The payoff was good for everyone," Atwood wrote on the tenth anniversary of the event. "The skiers had fun. The airlines had happy employees. Alyeska became world famous and attracted skiers from many nations."

Bob Atwood died in 1997.

The World Cup Giant Slalom

If the 1963 National Alpine Championships put Mount Alyeska on the skiing map, the 1973 Tesoro-Alaskan World Cup Giant Slalom cinched its reputation as one of the top racing mountains in the world.

It was Alaska's first major international competition and required a substantial organizational and financial investment to house, feed, and transport 160 racers and coaches and 40 members of the media. Under World Cup rules, "the supporting club is responsible for complete organization, funding and actual conduct of the individual races." Alyeska Ski Club, then headed by Judy Moerlen, was the sponsoring club.

More than one hundred volunteers pitched in to help out the all-Alaskan race committee that included Jay Burnett, chief of race; Mary Ellen Smalley, race secretary; Don Conrad, chief of course; Bud Carter, chief steward; Augie Reetz, chief of gatekeeping; and Don Simasko, Sam Hayes, Bill Scott, and Forest West, chief timer and calculations. Volunteers boot-packed the race course to harden the snowpack.

The organizing committee selected Paul Nattanguk, a Native artist from King Island, to produce the race awards. Nattanguk carved and polished ivory walrus tusks for the top three finishers in the men and women's races.

But it was a walrus oosik that captured the Austrian team's attention. Alyeska's Chris von Imhof took the team, including coach Tony Sailer and muscular downhill racer Annamarie Proell, for a visit to the Bird House bar, renowned then for the underwear that dangled from its ceiling and its wallpaper of business cards. Bartender Hugh Cruikshank regaled the visitors with his stories and displays, including the oosik, which he asked Proell to kiss. She did. When he informed her that it was the bone of a walrus penis, she reacted by kicking von Imhof and Sailer off their bar stools. "We were no match for her legs, which were the size of tree stumps," von Imhof said.

A competitor clears a gate at the 1973 Tesoro-Alaskan World Cup Giant Slalom competition, sponsored by the Alyeska Ski Club. Mountain manager Don Conrad laid out the race course, which competitors ranked as one of the most physically challenging in the world.

Don Conrad

▲ Don Conrad [ALYESKA RESORT]

▼ The crew constructing Chair 2 takes a break during the summer of 1972. The lift opened more ski terrain with reliably good snow conditions and enabled the resort to make its first profit. Crew members included Dave Gunderson, lift foreman (second from left); Angel Zopolos and Dave Scott, owner of Far North Ski Guides (third and fourth from left); Danny Jones and Al Hampton (seventh and eighth from left). [ALYESKA RESORT]

Don Conrad became a legend in his own time.

"Alyeska would never have made it without Conrad, who ran around with a wrench to fix the chairlift and a chainsaw to cut the trees," said long-time skier Per Bjorn-Roli.

"He made things go with very little money, doggedly snowplowing ahead, sometimes bending the rules by charging ahead without all the permits in hand," said Chris von Imhof, Alyeska's vice president and managing director.

"He always packed a chainsaw," said Larry Daniels, who succeeded Conrad as mountain manager. "It was his favorite tool."

"He used to ski down the mountain with a chainsaw running, cutting alders," said Mike Veatch, who has worked for Conrad for many years.

Conrad also worked more hours than two people combined, started the Mighty Mites ski program, and set the race courses for some of the biggest competitions in the world. But stories about Conrad tend to overlook his many positives and concentrate on his temper and his antics, like the first time von Imhof fired him.

"The outdoor swimming pool was the bane of our existence," Daniels said. "We couldn't get the chlorine levels right and it was June and Chris wanted the pool open. Conrad threw a bunch of chlorine into it and then shocked it, which turned the water all black. The two have words and within ten minutes, Conrad roars up in his truck, rocks and dust flying everywhere, and comes screaming into the lift shack, beating the daylights out of things, which was not unusual, but then he leaves with most of the tools."

It turned out that Conrad owned "most of the stuff we needed to run Alyeska." Conrad stayed gone for about a year.

Veatch likes to tell the tale of Tom Miller's revenge. "Miller was ski patrol director, a big, cowboy-type guy who used to get into it a lot. He wore a cap with a big pom-pom on it and Conrad wanted that pom-pom really bad. One night the two of them were tussling in the Sitzmark and went through the door into the liquor storeroom. I don't remember who won, but the pom-pom came off.

"Conrad always wore a hard hat, and one day he got real sick with a bad headache. It turned out that Miller had coated the inside of Conrad's sweatband with nitroglycerin from the dynamite we used."

Today Conrad operates a successful contracting business in Girdwood.

Bob Bursiel

He set out to fulfill a dream, not to help found a community, but thirty years after Bob Bursiel lay in his Colorado bed studying the Alaska maps plastered all over his ceiling, he could look back with a sense of accomplishment.

The little town he helped father boasted an extensive water and sewer system, a better school, a modern fire station, a vastly improved road link to Anchorage, and a proper anchor for its economy. He worked first with the Girdwood Community Club, which handled local problems until they became too expensive, and then with a more formal city government.

Girdwood incorporated September 20, 1961, with a mayor-city council form of government "to promote health and safety standards" and "speak with a stronger voice." The resort remained outside the city boundaries. Bursiel served as mayor of Girdwood for twelve of the fourteen years before it and the resort were absorbed into the Municipality of Anchorage.

But politics was the furthest thing from his mind when he loaded his wife, eleven-month-old baby, and a friend in his Jeep and headed for Alaska in 1948. The trip from Colorado took twenty-one days. They camped in the vehicle and ate what they could find. "Bunnies, squirrel, and once we ate crow," said his wife, Virginia.

The road north ended in Anchorage, so Bursiel walked along the Alaska Railroad track until he found the perfect spot in Girdwood. Jobs were at a premium in those days and Bursiel, a geologist, worked where he could—as a laborer, wagon-drill operator, and engineer on the Seward Highway construction; a school agent during Territorial days; and highway maintenance and avalanche research after statehood.

Bursiel was a founding member of the Alyeska Ski Corp. and helped punch in the first road to the mountain base and install the first rope tow. It was work he never regretted. "I think everybody recognizes that if the ski resort wasn't here, there would be nothing here."

Bursiel died in 1996.

Parade marshals Virginia and Bob Bursiel travel the route of the 1988 Girdwood Forest Fair parade. Bob helped organize the movement to incorporate Girdwood as a city and served twelve years as its mayor.

[KEN GRAHAM]

Avalanches

▼ Alyeska's Chris von Imhof [right] has a few words with mountain ranger O'Leary on April 4, 1969, after O'Leary's avalanche control efforts inadvertently set off an avalanche that damaged the base terminal tower and forced an early closure to the season. [ALYESKA RESORT]

Skier Eddie Gendzwill and mountain ranger Chuck O'Leary started up the mountain after a night of high winds.

"We got halfway to the sundeck and decided to head across the south slope," Gendzwill said. "I was 150 feet behind Chuck. Suddenly, as I got halfway across the slope, here comes this huge avalanche right on top of me.

▲ Mountain ranger Chuck O'Leary aims a 75 mm gun at snow-loaded slopes in 1970, ready to fire in order to clear them of potential avalanches. [ALYESKA RESORT]

▲▲ In the late 1990s the resort began to transition to 105 mm recoilless guns, thanks to help from U.S. Senator Ted Stevens. [ALYESKA RESORT]

"There I was, knocked over and rolling inside the snow. Then all of a sudden I found myself lying on top of an alder bush and that saved my life. It wasn't long before Chuck spotted me and asked what I was doing. 'Sunning myself,' was my answer."

Alyeska is a class A avalanche area due to steep terrain and ample snowfall, but its avalanche control program is considered one of the best in the world. "I take a lot of pride in our program," said Chris von Imhof, Alyeska's vice president and managing director. "We have good, dedicated people and we do what they tell us, even if that means closing down the mountain."

There have been close calls, particularly in the early days when ski patrollers used sticks of dynamite [instead of the artillery shells now used] to purposely set off avalanches and control the danger. Avalanche expert Dave Hamre remembers the day Max's Mountain let loose in the midst of an employee party despite repeated dynamiting earlier in the day. "It was May 1, 1980, and it went really big, almost into the day lodge, and there were employees all over the mountain."

Avalanches can play havoc with the Seward Highway. Five major avalanches blocked the highway for days in 1979, stranding 225 people at the resort and hundreds of others throughout the valley. *The Anchorage Times* reported that Alyeska spread out a buffet of roast pork, prime rib, chicken, salads, and desserts for its guests and that the liquor stores ran dry. Wilbur's Flying Service ran a brisk business flying people out—five at a time for fifteen dollars a seat—in its Cessna 206.

▲ Billows of snow rise upward as an avalanche thunders off a ridge near Girdwood in the spring of 1979. During this period, avalanches closed the Seward Highway for five days, stranding many skiers. Wilbur's Flying Service evacuated skiers for fifteen dollars each.

◄ Five helicopters park on the Seward Highway at the entrance to Glacier Valley ready to ferry people in and out of the community. A series of massive avalanches that began Super Bowl Sunday 2001 stranded Girdwood for a week. The community lost power about halfway through the ordeal. [Eric Teela]

4

Where East Meets West

"We have arrived," thought Chris von Imhof as he stood at the top of Mount Alyeska with Yoshiaki Tsutsumi, the resort's new owner.

Tsutsumi pointed down the North Face and asked if the resort could purchase the land at the base. "Possibly," responded von Imhof, Alyeska's vice president and managing director.

"Well, that's where we'll build the tram and hotel," Tsutsumi said.

A tram costs ten to twelve million dollars, so von Imhof knew that "this was the start of something big."

Tsutsumi's company, the Seibu Group, ended up investing $200 million in Alyeska, and von Imhof later took a ten-year detour to Hawaii, where he opened two Prince Hotels for the company.

The centerpiece of the Seibu investment is the 307-room Alyeska Prince Hotel and the mile-long, sixty-passenger tram. But it took ten years, miles of red tape, and a major struggle by Larry Daniels before the hotel opened in 1994. Daniels stepped in as construction manager when von Imhof was sent off to Hawaii.

Although Anchorage lost its bids to host the

Lights of the Alyeska Prince Hotel cast a warm glow into the night sky. The 307-room facility is the only Alaska hotel to gain an AAA Four Diamond Rating. The architecture mimics the surrounding Chugach Mountain Range.

Winter Olympics, athletes who developed their skills at Alyeska made big impressions at the Games. Hilary Lindh won silver in the women's downhill, Tommy Moe became the first American skier to take two medals during a single Olympics, Rosey Fletcher showed the world how to run a slalom on a snowboard, and ski-jumping coach Karl Eid saw his best student, Alan Alborn, fly farther than any other American

Alyeska hosted a number of important races, including the 1981 National Alpine Championships, the 1989 World Junior Alpine Championships, and the 2001 Special Olympics World Winter Games. The resort worked with Doug Keil, an extraordinary Alaskan who turned a personal loss into a program called Challenge Alaska that helps people with disabilities enjoy the great outdoors.

Girdwood rubbed shoulders with Tinseltown when producers of *The Runaway Train* chose the town as home base for making the film, and the resort sponsored a Celebrity Sports Invitational. The community greeted Ken Osuna and his new newspaper and bid adieu to one of its favorite characters, Stumpy Faulkner.

Yoshiaki Tsutsumi

The World's Richest Man

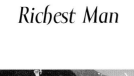

The smile said it all. Yoshiaki Tsutsumi surveyed his new investment and pronounced that he was pleased.

Two hundred million dollars had transformed a struggling little resort into a four-season destination, complete with Alaska's only AAA Four Diamond hotel and restaurant, a sixty-passenger aerial tram, new day lodge, and two new quad chairlifts, plus a new snowmaking system and equipment to keep the slopes groomed.

Chris von Imhof no longer had to rob Peter to pay Paul. It was a remarkable transformation financed and orchestrated by an extraordinary man with a distinctly non-American perspective. Yoshiaki Tsutsumi thinks in decades, not the next quarter, and believes a promise made is a debt unpaid.

Of course it helped to be the richest man in the world, with closely held assets, who reports only to himself.

"Any American investor would have walked away," said von Imhof, Alyeska's vice president and managing director.

The world had changed dramatically from the day in 1980 that Alaska Airlines sold Alyeska Resort to Seibu for $6.5 million to the time the Alyeska Prince opened in 1994. Anchorage lost its international passenger flights, including direct air service from Japan, when the Cold War thawed and Russian air space opened. "The company had expected 15 to 20 percent of its guests would be Japanese," von Imhof said.

Alaska lost its bid to host the 1992 and then the

◄◄ Alyeska owner Yoshiaki Tsutsumi [fourth from left] visited in 1981 to select the location for the Alyeska Prince Hotel and tram. Alyeska's Chris von Imhof is at far right. [Alyeska Resort]

◄ The Alyeska Aerial Tram ascends one mile from the Alyeska Prince Hotel at the base of Mount Alyeska to the 2,300-foot Glacier Terminal, carrying sixty passengers at a time. The ride takes three and a half minutes for skiers in winter but slows to half speed in summer so tourists can appreciate the sweeping views of Glacier Valley and Turnagain Arm.

1994 Winter Olympics. Alyeska would have been the alpine venue and in the world's spotlight.

Alaska's economy had fallen apart, and then Japan's began to slide, severely impacting Tsutsumi. As *Forbes Magazine* reported in 2002: "The world's richest man in 1990, this land baron's net worth has dwindled from $16 billion to $2.5 billion along with Japan's real estate market."

And there were all the delays and red tape. The Municipality of Anchorage, of which Alyeska is a part, had never permitted a luxury hotel and tram in the wilderness. Gaining permission was an excruciating process that added years and millions to the project's cost.

"Alaska is fortunate our owner had money, confidence, and a long-term vision," von Imhof said.

A natural athlete who enjoys golf and skiing, Tsutsumi has the physique of a boxer. He won

Tokyo's first 400-meter relay footrace after the end of World War II, and the 800-meter a year later. He went on to become chairman of the skiing and skating federations, vice president of the Japan Amateur Sports Association, and a member of the Japanese Olympics Committee. He was instrumental in bringing the Winter Olympics to Nagano.

He also introduced ice hockey to Japan and owns one of the country's top baseball teams, the Seibu Lions. His sports interests perfectly fit his business interests.

Tsutsumi followed in the footsteps of his father, the late Yasujiro Tsutsumi, who rose from obscurity to become one of Japan's most powerful entrepreneurs and political figures. A former Speaker of the House, he, too, took a long-term view, advising his son to always plan a decade in advance.

"My father's teaching was, first, number one,

The New Year's Eve torchlight parade lights its way down Mount Alyeska. Longtime coach Bud Gibbs first organized the event for his Mighty Mites ski program but anyone who wants to ski down with a torch in hand can participate. Fireworks follow the parade.

borrow money, and next, buy land. By which he meant, once you've bought land you've done 99 percent of your business," Tsutsumi once told a reporter.

"My job is simply to put paint on my father's work. But if I only did that, the business would not progress, so in order to perpetuate the Seibu group I buy land for the future. My father's rule was always never to touch manufacturing. I just follow my father's way."

Tsutsumi used his father's land to create a leisure industry so widespread that one could live in a Seibu apartment, travel on a Seibu train, stay at a Seibu hotel, shop at a Seibu store, holiday at a Seibu resort, and have fun at a Seibu ski area, golf course, or skating rink.

"He looked at the soaring snow-covered peaks and saw magnificent skiing country," wrote one journalist. "He looked at the plains and woodlands around the foothills and saw lush green golf courses."

He also realized that postwar Japan was emerging from years of struggle and that its middle class now had the time and the yen for fun.

His first challenge came from his father, who wanted to lure visitors to Japan's Karuizawa region in the winter. Ice skating, concluded Tsutsumi, who built a 400-meter indoor rink where people could glide in comfort. It was an immediate success. The five thousand people who showed up the first day after opening quickly grew to thirty thousand a day.

Tsutsumi then introduced the concept of a seaside resort on land his father owned in Oiso. For his college thesis, he created plans for a luxurious hotel with a large, freshwater pool 328 feet long and 164 feet wide, surrounded by intricate landscaping. His father built the hotel and the pool, and crowds of guests immediately came.

Tsutsumi wanted to hook the Japanese on skiing so he could develop mountain land that he and his father owned. He built a small ski area just outside downtown Tokyo, at the end of one of the family's rail lines. It had a roof, two single chairlifts, and used chipped ice for snow.

"Marvelous business plan," said Alyeska's Larry Daniels. "He first created a bunch of skiers who quickly outgrew this tiny area, then provided them with Naeba, which became a screaming success. Upwards of forty thousand skiers on acreage just twice the size of Alyeska."

"His greatest enthusiasm is for new projects, the planning, design, and execution," said von Imhof. "He calls all his consultants together and creates such a whirlwind of activity I call him Mr. Tsunami."

Standing on Mount Alyeska with von Imhof, Tsutsumi personally selected the site for the Alyeska Prince Hotel and tram and immediately involved himself with the smallest detail. "He once kept a Japan Airlines jet waiting while he redrew the circular driveway at the hotel's entrance," von Imhof said.

"He is highly intelligent, the visionary during the design stage who would take the professionals' ideas and improve them," said Daniels, who oversaw construction of the Alyeska Prince Hotel.

Tsutsumi is a taskmaster who is used to getting his way. The hotel model that worked so well in Japan contained potentially fatal flaws for Alaska, where the busy season is summer and providing space for business meetings is essential for success. "He saw it as a winter facility," explained Daniels, who had the delicate task of persuading Tsutsumi to add meeting and banquet facilities, along with a swimming pool. "Our strong summer and convention season has been a real surprise for him."

Daniels said Tsutsumi allows his properties to operate independently and to retain operating profits for additional capital improvements. "He's not necessarily looking for double-digit returns," Daniels said. "He hasn't sold any of his underperforming properties and he continues to build new ones, albeit at a slower pace and more cost-conscious. Failure isn't in his vocabulary and he's an old-fashioned Japanese who really does think long-term."

"Alaska is fortunate," von Imhof said, "that Mr. Tsutsumi made such a major investment in this state."

▲ Chris von Imhof and Kochi Hayashi announce the sale of Alyeska resort to Seibu Alaska, a subsidiary of the Japanese leisure conglomerate, at a September 1980 press conference. Hayashi was director and executive vice president of Seibu Alaska. The sale set off a real estate frenzy that saw Girdwood lot prices almost double during 1980.

▲ A snowmaking machine sprays the white stuff onto an Alyeska run in 1983. Snowmaking is available on nearly half of the resort's ski terrain, including more than two dozen trails.

The Alyeska Prince Hotel

The Alyeska Prince Hotel snuggles into the base of the mountain, surrounded by hanging glaciers and towering spruce trees. The chateau-style architecture, designed by Sasaki Associates of Boston, mimics the mighty Chugach Mountain Range down to its multihued gray and ochre coloration that blends so well into the surrounding countryside.

On one side a pond provides ice skating during the winter and a bubbling fountain in the summer. A

► Miles of cherry paneling give a sense of warmth to the interior of the Alyeska Prince Hotel. The hotel, which opened in 1994, includes a fitness center and offers northern lights wake-up calls for its guests.

tram and chairlift connect this ski-in/ski-out hotel with Mount Alyeska.

Alaska's only AAA Four Diamond hotel, the Alyeska Prince offers an interior that exudes warmth, with miles of cherry paneling, huge fireplaces, and comfortable sofas and chairs. *Snow Country* magazine voted it the best hotel over one hundred rooms designed for a ski property; the *Connoisseur's Guide to the Best Hotels* awarded it its Connoisseur's Choice award in 2001.

The hotel's beginnings were anything but graceful and beautiful. Originally planned as a 128-room, six-story property, the design and location encountered problems with municipal regulators who had no experience with construction of a luxury resort in the middle of nowhere. The situation grew so serious that Seibu withdrew its construction application in 1983 and instead proposed a fifty-room addition to the Nugget Inn.

Technical problems with expanding the Nugget brought a new design for the Prince Hotel that featured 307 guest rooms, a fitness center, restaurants, upscale shops, and 15,000 square feet of event space to accommodate groups up to 450.

The Prince finally opened in August 1994, millions of dollars over budget due to construction delays and permit problems. Its inaugural winter was abysmal, with little snow and few guests. Occupancy averaged 24 percent the first year, with room rates priced beyond the local market and marketing efforts limited. Three times the hotel reduced its staff.

Finally, Chris von Imhof, who had been sent to Hawaii by Seibu to work on hotel projects there, asked to return to "my mountain."

The Seibu Investment

The timing was right when Alaska Airlines told Chris von Imhof to find a new owner for Alyeska Resort.

Japan was banker to the world, ready to launch an international spending spree. It was the largest creditor nation on the globe with assets of $350 billion while the United States was the largest debtor with debts of $650 billion.

Alaska Airlines had a marketing agent in Japan who helped von Imhof put together a sales brochure in Japanese and set up a meeting with Seibu, one of the world's largest leisure-industry conglomerates. Seibu expressed an interest and sent a four-person team to Alyeska in April 1980. "There was a hotel expert, a ski expert, a lift expert who spent days looking the property over," von Imhof recalled.

"We hosted the inspection team the final night at my home with a big pot of king crab and kids crawling all over the floor. They seemed to really enjoy the informal setting but one inquired very politely if I might have some soy sauce. I pulled a big bottle from the pantry and that cinched the deal."

Well, not exactly—but the Seibu team did report favorably to its owner and a deal was signed October 1 with the stipulation that von Imhof be part of the package.

"We thought things would move fast, but they didn't," he said. Seibu asked von Imhof to move to Hawaii to open the 310-room Maui Prince Hotel and then to Honolulu to build the 550-room Hawaiian Prince Hotel Waikiki. Both properties featured "beautiful beaches, wonderful golf courses, and great weather.

"This was a ten-year absence with pay that beat the old days with Chair 1."

But von Imhof missed "his" mountain, and when he discovered that the Alyeska Prince Hotel was struggling, he asked to go home. Things were bleak at the Prince, with an inadequate marketing program and room rates set so high that Alaskans simply stayed home and the critical summer cruise ship business said no thanks.

Von Imhof laid out a marketing plan and reported a $1.5 million operating profit two years later. "I was treated like a hero when I visited Japan."

Seibu continues to build new projects, though at a slower rate than previously. It completed the world's largest gondola in 2002, connecting four mountaintops in the Japanese Alps. Seibu holdings included seventy-nine Prince hotels, twenty-three golf courses, amusement parks, skating rinks, the Seibu Railway Line, Seibu Construction, and more.

▲ Seibu completes the new day lodge just in time for the 1989 World Junior Championships.

▼ The Alyeska Aerial Tram moves at speeds up to twenty-six miles an hour. It operates on a weight-counterweight system: when one car goes up, the other car comes down. The Four Diamond rated Seven Glaciers Restaurant is located in its terminus.

Jill and Jim Veatch

Jill Veatch

Jim and Jill Veatch are consummate opposites—the happy-go-lucky ski bum and the classy lady who makes sure every "i" is dotted and "t" crossed.

Jill takes care of top management in her work for Alyeska's Chris von Imhof; hubby Jim rides herd on the outlaws as a security officer at the resort. Together they are parents of a deaf son with a penchant for jumping off high places on skis.

They met at the resort's Sitzmark Bar on Christmas Eve 1980, both suffering a case of holiday blahs—he the son of a preacher man who came to Alaska to build a church; she on an uncharted track with a man who had misled her. The attraction was instantaneous—and they went on to become Mr. and Mrs.

Jill says she loves "her life and this amazing little town," even though her house is unfinished after all these many years. She has more exciting things on her plate—like planning a repeat of the Celebrity Sports Invitational at Alyeska that led to her lunch at a London pub with Pierce Brosnan.

Jim Veatch

Jim has been at Alyeska so long they call him the Mountain Man.

He lived in a tent and rowed to work each day across a pond when he was "young and dumb." Strapped forty pounds of dynamite on his back and went looking for avalanche hazards to blow away. Climbed halfway up the mountain to string Christmas lights [later they used a helicopter]. Took a flight to San Francisco for lunch. And blew his finger off ten days after he got married.

Now that he's "older and smarter," he dresses up in funny clothes and plays Santa. He's gentle and funny, with a full beard that doesn't need to be grayed when he dresses as St. Nick.

"Jim's always been Mr. Cool, Mr. Happy," says general manager Larry Daniels of the Alyeska Ski Area. "He's done just about everything on the mountain, from running Chair 1 for the tourists to managing the bar, and he's done it well."

Back in the days when he had hair, Veatch was "anything but orderly," Daniels said. Veatch hounded Daniels to let him drive the bulldozer and Daniels finally told him to go check the fuel. "He did and tells me the tank is full, which I know it isn't," Daniels said. "He had checked the radiator instead, so I suggested he needed to learn which end was which before we turned him loose."

To which Veatch responds, "That's what you get when they don't train you."

The snow ranger at the time thought Veatch was not responsible enough to man the gun used to set off avalanches as a safety precaution. But when a new ranger showed up and said he needed a gunner, Veatch said, "Let's go." Veatch developed into one of the best snow safety men on the mountain.

"Where else do you get paid to shoot artillery and no one shoots back at you?" Veatch asked.

Larry Daniels

Larry Daniels came to Alyeska on a three-month contract more than thirty years ago. His job was construction of Chair 3, which offers access to Alyeska's beginner slopes.

"It was a pretty interesting time with seniority measured in days," he said. Congress had just given the green light to building the trans-Alaska oil pipeline, then the largest privately financed project in history. At peak construction more than twenty-eight thousand people worked on the $8 billion venture for wages that few companies could match.

"Within the first month, only one other outside crew person had been there longer than me," Daniels said.

Daniels describes himself as a "good old-fashioned ski bum" from Washington state who wanted to stay in the ski business. "At most ski areas it takes twenty years to become mountain manager," Daniels said. He made it in four, and today holds the title of general manager, Alyeska Ski Area and The Anchorage Golf Course.

It's been a good ride for Daniels, who married the sweetheart he met at White Pass area in Washington state and had the pleasure of raising a family in the "tight-knit, neat little community" of Girdwood.

Larry Daniels takes a flying bungee jump off the Alyeska Aerial Tram to scout a location for an MTV shoot in 1996. Daniels, general manager of Alyeska Ski Area and The Anchorage Golf Course, says he runs a pretty "conservative" operation—but the resort is adding more adventure-based activities, including rock climbing and glacier walking.

Alyeska Skiing

Mount Alyeska offers more than 2,500 vertical feet of the best steeps, deeps, bumps, and jumps in North America. It's a mountain that skis bigger than it is; Olympic gold medalist Tommy Moe calls it "so sweet."

Skiing magazine rated it number one in North America for snow and number six for steeps, calling the terrain "well-proportioned." Most experts rank it in the top three "tough mountains" in North America.

At 250 feet, it has the lowest base elevation of any ski resort in the world. While skiers experience no altitude-related headaches or breathlessness, they must be ready to encounter every snow condition that exists in wintertime climates.

The mountain receives as much as 1,100 inches of snow each year, with a 742-inch average. Ski season typically stretches from mid-November through mid-April, with weekend skiing through Memorial Day as conditions permit.

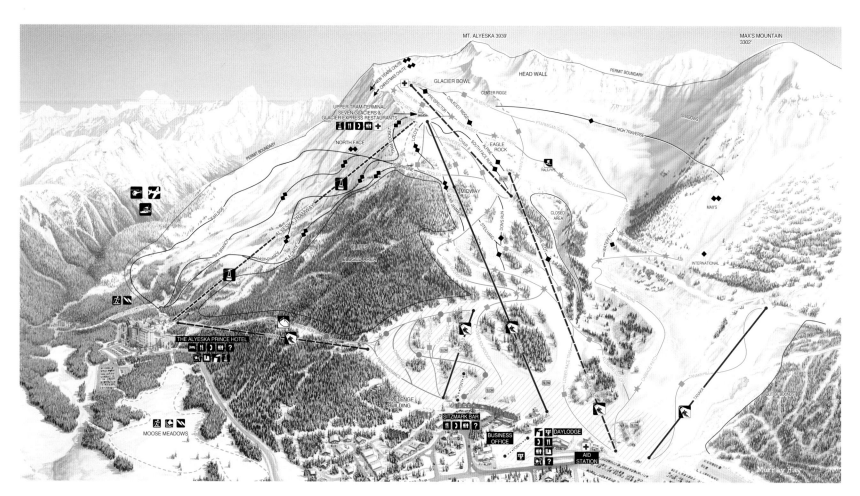

Championships and Champions

In a dramatic testament to the strength of Alyeska's racing program, eight of the thirty-five members of the 1981 U.S. Ski Team were graduates of the Mighty Mites program at Alyeska, as were two of the coaches.

Alyeska hosted the 1981 National Alpine Championships, which drew top skiers including brothers Steve and Phil Mahre, Christin Cooper, and Tamara McKinney. More than half of the twenty Alaskans who ran the downhill at these championships came through the Alyeska Ski Club program, including Marc Eid and Brian Burnett.

In 1989, Alyeska played host to the World Junior Alpine Championships. The U.S. team captured eight medals, the most ever, including two golds for hometown favorite Tommy Moe.

▲ The Mahre brothers of Washington state were overall champions at the 1981 National Alpine Championships, held at Alyeska. Phil [left], fresh from winning his first overall World Cup title, won the giant slalom; brother Steve won the slalom.

◄ Junior Alyeska racer Kelly Johnson leads in the Japanese delegation during opening ceremonies of the 1989 World Junior Alpine Championships at Alyeska. The U.S. team captured eight medals, including two golds for hometown favorite Tommy Moe. [ALYESKA RESORT]

Paul Crews Jr.

▲ A heavily bearded Paul Crews Jr. stands outside the cabin he and friends Keith Tryck, Bob Clark, and Jerry Wallace built on the banks of the Yukon River.

[GAIL PATTISON]

▶ Paul Crews Jr. [CREWS FAMILY]

He was the first homegrown Alaskan to make the U.S. Ski Team—lean and wiry with nerves of steel.

After winning All-American status at Western State College [Colorado] in 1970, Paul Crews spent two years with the U.S. Ski Team and two more on the World Pro Skiing Circuit. He went from there into a variety of enterprises, ski-related and otherwise, which allowed him to keep coaching.

In 1975, Crews was put in charge of the Alyeska racing program, taking time out in 1978, 1980, and 1981 to serve as U.S. Ski Team associate coach and Europa Cup coach. He took over the alpine program at the University of Alaska Anchorage in 1983 and coached the Seawolves for almost two decades.

Back in the 1970s, Crews took off on a grand adventure with his childhood buddy Keith Tryck.

Over a period of four years, the two friends, along with photographer Bob Clark and logger Jerry Wallace, traveled four thousand miles by raft, by ski, by dogsled. Their epic journey was captured in the book *Yukon Passage* and in one of the most popular television specials ever produced by National Geographic.

Tryck said conflict resolution became a real skill during their Yukon odyssey. "Here you have four strong men in a twelve-by-fourteen tent. We quickly developed patterns for solving disagreements."

Crews put this skill to good use during his long coaching career, which produced a number of national champions. He's now retired in Girdwood, still working an occasional construction job. As he likes to say, "Old skiers never go away."

Super-racers

More top-notch ski racers come off Alyeska than from any other mountain its size in North America.

"Not only is the mountain challenging, it throws every condition possible at you," said longtime coach Bud Gibbs. "You take off with a little Rocky Mountain champagne powder, then Snoqualmie slush, and end up on Eastern ice—and that's on every run."

▲ Alyeska-trained Kjersti Bjorn-Roli shows off her winning downhill racing form. A member of the U.S. Ski Team from the season of 1992-93 to the 2000-2001 season, she came tantalizingly close to the Olympics, but injuries and three knee operations forced an early retirement from racing. Alyeska has produced more speed champions than any other mountain its size.
[BJORN-ROLI FAMILY]

▲ Mike Makar [GLACIER CREEK ACADEMY]
▶ ▲ Megan Gerety

Tommy Moe

When Tommy Moe stood on the top step in Lillehammer, Norway, it was "the ultimate life experience.

"The timing was perfect, my technique was solid, and my mental outlook was all or nothing."

At the 1994 Lillehammer Olympics, Moe won gold in the downhill, then took silver in the super G on his birthday four days later. He became the first U.S. alpine skier to win two medals in the same Olympics. He followed this remarkable performance with a World Cup win in the giant slalom and other top-ten finishes that season.

"The Olympic experience is one I would never trade," he said, "skiing at premier ski locations and representing your country in one of the oldest races known to man."

Moe spent twelve years on the World Cup circuit, retiring in 1998 after a series of injuries. "I've had a great time in my career, traveled the world."

Moe arrived in Girdwood when he was thirteen and enrolled in Glacier Creek Academy. "Tommy was good when he got here," said longtime racing coach Bud Gibbs. "He showed the sixteen-year-olds just how good a thirteen-year-old could be."

Alaska and Moe seemed made for each other. An outdoorsman at heart, he returns annually to hunt and fish and is involved with Class V Whitewater, a rafting and kayaking guide service based in Girdwood, and Chugach Powder Guides, a heli-skiing operation. He also started a weekend ski race at Alyeska, the Tommy Moe Invitational, which sees about 150 kids each year.

Home these days is Jackson Hole, Wyoming, where he is ski ambassador at Jackson Hole Mountain Resort and a popular figure on the celebrity ski circuit. But he returned to his roots the summer of 2003 when he married fellow Olympian Megan Gerety on top of Mount Alyeska.

▲ 1989 World Junior Champion Tommy Moe [U.S. Ski Team]

◄ With his trademark smile, Olympic champion Tommy Moe meets with junior racers in April 1992. Moe sponsors the Tommy Moe Invitational, a weekend race at Alyeska that draws 150 kids each year. Moe won Olympic gold in the downhill and silver in the super giant slalom in 1994. He now lives in Jackson, Wyoming, but remains involved in a Girdwood-based helicopter ski operation and a rafting company. [Ken Graham]

Hilary Lindh

If there's a ski racer who clearly has all the right stuff, it's Hilary Lindh.

Born and raised in Juneau, Lindh went on to become an Olympic and World champion, but when it came time to retire, she didn't hesitate. She left competitive racing and earned a bachelor of science degree at the University of Utah, where she served on the board of trustees for the Salt Lake City Olympic Committee and on its environmental advisory committee. She went on to the master of science program at the Centre for Applied Conservation Research at the University of British Columbia, where she studied ecological impacts of development and recreation in alpine areas.

Lindh's academic achievements come as no surprise to those who knew her at Mount Alyeska, where she spent many days training and racing. "She was quiet, the model daughter who had it all together," recalled longtime ski coach Bud Gibbs.

"I watched Hilary come here when she was eleven and twelve and run a downhill race and beat the sixteen- and seventeen-year-old boys. A great girl, so strong, so fluid, so very graceful."

Lindh went from Alyeska to the World Junior Championships, where she won gold in downhill. She was a three-time Olympian, winning silver in the 1992 Albertville games and placing seventh in Lillehammer. She spent thirteen years on the U.S. Ski Team and is a five-time U.S. downhill champion.

Lindh's parents live in Juneau, where she returns annually to visit family and friends during the holidays and to occasionally teach a ski clinic on her home hill at Eaglecrest.

Sporting an Alyeska headband, Olympic ski racer Hilary Lindh takes a photo break. She was born and raised in Juneau and often trained at Alyeska. A veteran of three Winter Olympics, she won silver in downhill at the 1992 Games. [KEN GRAHAM]

Rosey Fletcher

Her smile is as big as her record: Girdwood's own Rosey Fletcher, one of the world's leading snowboarders.

"A very positive role model and a good ambassador for Girdwood," said *Turnagain Times* publisher Ken Osuna.

"Friendly, determined, and a very good alpine racer," said her former Mighty Mites coach Bud Gibbs.

Fletcher put on her first pair of skis at age three but switched to snowboarding when she was fifteen. She won the silver medal in the 1999 World Championships plus four World Cups and ended the season ranked fourth in the world. Two years later she was again second in the 2001 World Championships and finished the season with seven World Cup wins and a third-place World Cup ranking. By 2003 she had won three golds and two silvers at the U.S. Nationals.

Fletcher was the first snowboarder named to the 1998 Olympic team and was chosen again for the 2002 Olympics. Her events are giant slalom, parallel giant slalom, and slalom.

"Success," she said, "is defined by a love for your sport in a way that is contagious to others. You can measure success by the smiles you put on other people's faces."

A sometimes reporter for various Alaska newspapers, the tall blonde woman with All-American looks wants to become a TV sports commentator when she hangs up her racing board.

Girdwood native Rosey Fletcher takes a turn during snowboard competition at the 2002 Winter Olympics at Salt Lake City. She grew up skiing Mount Alyeska, where she was a member of the Mighty Mites team. Alyeska was slow to open its slopes to snowboarders, so Fletcher didn't start snowboarding until she was fifteen years old.
[2002 WINTER OLYMPIC GAMES]

Challenge Alaska

Doug Keil lost the life he first loved when he was fourteen years old. He and some friends were exploring an abandoned gold mine near Juneau when they found a rusty power pole that appeared dormant. Keil was starting to climb it when 23,000 volts of electricity racked his body.

He survived, but the toll was extreme. Keil's abdomen, kidney, and intestines were seared and he lost his left arm and left leg. He spent two years in the University of Washington Medical Center, and when he went home, he fell victim to substance abuse.

His parents grew increasingly desperate and finally, when he was twenty, sent him to a ski instruction course for the disabled in Winter Park, Colorado. It was a natural fit for a person who loved baseball, hockey, track, and skiing.

He grew ever faster and became the national disabled ski champion in the late 1970s, and then conquered the world when he won gold medals in slalom and giant slalom at the 1980 International Ski Championship in Norway.

Keil returned to Alaska determined to share his experiences with others. He helped found Challenge Alaska in 1981 "to regenerate the individual and the family of the individual."

Challenge Alaska provides outdoor activities for the physically challenged. The organization offers lessons and ski equipment at Alyeska during the winter, and fishing, sea kayaking, canoeing, camping, horseback riding, hiking, and river rafting during the summer. The group serves more than one thousand Alaskans.

"To get outside, to participate in some sort of outdoor activity, makes life that much more worth living," Keil says.

Challenge Alaska built a 9,000-square-foot ski chalet adjacent to Alyeska's Chair 3. Constructed primarily with donated labor and materials, the two-story building of paneled wood and stone pillars is 100 percent wheelchair accessible.

About one hundred disabled skiers participate in the program at Alyeska as either sit-skiers in sleds or as stand-up skiers on one or two skis plus outriggers, which are poles equipped with skis. Sit-skiers either tuck their bodies into sleds or use specially designed mono-skis. They ride the chairlift with the assistance of a friend, and then shoot down the mountain using ski poles to brake and regulate speed, and weight distribution to steer.

▲ Doug Keil [Doug Keil]

◄ A sit-skier participates in the 1995 Challenge Alaska Skiathon. Challenge Alaska runs an adaptive ski program from its International Sports, Recreation, and Education Center near the base of Chair 3 at Alyeska. The program helps people with disabilities enjoy summer and winter outdoor activities. [Greg Martin]

The Special Olympics

It was called a force of light and love that changed the Anchorage area forever, for the better: the 2001 Special Olympics World Winter Games Alaska.

The games brought 2,400 athletes and coaches to Anchorage from sixty-nine countries and was the biggest winter sporting event in the state's history. Some six thousand people volunteered and thousands more showed up to cheer on the athletes who have developmental disabilities.

A total of 288 athletes from thirty-three countries participated in the alpine skiing competition at Alyeska. One of the medal-winning competitors was David McBroom of Redmond, Washington, whose life had been saved through an Alaska family's organ donation of their dead child's heart.

Celebrities cheered on McBroom and the other racers. Actor Arnold Schwarzenegger and his wife, TV journalist Maria Shriver, posed for photographs and met with the teams. Olympic medalist Billy Kidd was helping all over the mountain as were Girdwood's favorite sisters, Olympic snowboarder Rosey Fletcher and Kate Fletcher, who hopes to beat her big sister some day.

Richard Camilleri, Jenna Elbert, and Rhea Racaza cheer on giant slalom competitors during the 2001 Special Olympics World Winter Games Alaska. A total of 288 athletes from thirty-three nations participated in the alpine competition at Alyeska. [BILL ROTH, *Anchorage Daily News*]

Karl Eid

Coach Karl Eid's best student, Alan Alborn, out-jumped every other American and finished eleventh in the world at the 2002 Winter Olympics despite a nagging injury. This coach who has raised the international profile of the sport of ski jumping was ninety-three years old at the time.

Since he first arrived in Anchorage in 1959, Eid has taught hundreds of Alaskans how to lift off a ski ramp, lean forward, and fly. Some fly farther than others—like Alborn, who started skiing at age two and began jumping at age nine in the Karl Eid program on the twenty-meter jump near Anchorage's Hilltop Ski Area.

Alborn retired in the spring of 2003 after winning his fifth national title. He had the best U.S. jumping results in a decade during the 2002 season, posting three top-ten finishes on the World Cup tour and extending his own national distance record when he went 221.5 meters in Slovenia.

Eid, who was born in Germany of Norwegian heritage, took his first jump in 1908 at his ancestral home of Eid's Fjord. He teamed up with a group of fellow jumpers who shared a pair of boots and skis. "It was junk," he once told a reporter. "We were going fifty, sixty, seventy meters and the boots were falling off."

Eid met Alyeska's Chris von Imhof in Garmisch, where Eid coached the 1936 Norwegian and German Olympic teams. Their friendship remained close over the years and culminated in realization of Eid's long-held dream of recognizing Alaska's Olympians and those who helped support them. The project is called the Golden Book and von Imhof introduced the first one in 2003.

In Anchorage, Eid was an associate professor of food technology at Anchorage Community College until circulatory problems necessitated his retirement. A blood clot forced doctors to amputate his right leg in 1995.

Eid coached his son, Marc, to be a good jumper but a better skier. Marc once held the title for the world's longest jump on alpine skis off of natural terrain—a jump known as a gelandesprung. He soared 268 feet at Alyeska in 1984. Marc went on to ski for the University of Alaska Anchorage and compete in a World Cup downhill at Aspen.

▲ Karl Eid

▲ Karl Eid, at left in the tan jacket, poses with his 1995 Alaska Nordic Jumping Team at Hilltop Ski Area in Anchorage. Hilltop's Karl Eid Ski Jump Complex includes a 15-meter lighted jump, a 40-meter lighted jump, and a 60-meter lighted jump. [ERIC TEELA]

95

The Stars

The guest list was loaded with celebrities, including Pierce Brosnan, William Shatner, astronaut Buzz Aldrin, and the woman who captured everyone's heart, sex adviser Ruth Westheimer, better known as Dr. Ruth.

"It was really fun," recalled Alyeska's Jill Veatch, who helped organize the 1998 Celebrity Sports Invitational. "Your typical Girdwood experience. Arrival day was ugly and black but the next three days were bluebird."

The celebrities dined well. One evening's menu was "nouveau native" and featured sautéed sheefish croquettes with roasted pepper aioli, musk ox and venison roasts carved to order, salmon caviar, caribou stew, and Alaska wild berry cobbler.

"Dr. Ruth was the neatest little lady," Veatch said. "She had to have a tall, handsome ski guide."

Other celebrities included Alan Thicke of the *Growing Pains* TV show, actress Shari Belafonte, *West Wing* vice president Tim Matheson, actress Mimi Rogers, comedian Jim Belushi, and musician Bobby Kimball.

Sex therapist Dr. Ruth Westheimer gets up-close and personal with TV and film star Pierce Brosnan during the 1998 Celebrity Sports Invitational at Alyeska. The celebrities participated in dual giant slalom races, a sled dog tournament, and a cross-country ski relay. [JOHN TRAUTNER]

The Big Screen

Tinseltown it's not, but Girdwood has played a starring role in three movies.

Girdwood served as home base for *Runaway Train*, the 1985 film starring Jon Voight and Eric Roberts, who picked up Oscar nominations for their roles.

Voight and Roberts play prison inmates who escape through a drain tunnel and then blunder onto a runaway train with only three people aboard: the convicts themselves and a railroad worker who is powerless to stop the train. The action sequences are stunning, even by today's standards, as the characters climb the sides of the ice-covered locomotive while the train crashes through barriers and other trains.

During filming, three helicopter crew members were killed in a crash in Portage Valley, near Girdwood.

In 1983 the Walt Disney Company sent a crew to Girdwood to shoot a segment of *America the Beautiful* that featured sled dogs. The show played for years in Disneyland's Tomorrowland.

The first feature-length film shot entirely in Alaska was set primarily in Girdwood: Cap Lathrop's 1924 black-and-white melodrama *The Chechahcos*.

Actor Jon Voight clings to the undercarriage of a railcar in the movie *The Runaway Train,* filmed primarily along the railroad tracks between Girdwood and Whittier. Voight, who was nominated for an Oscar for his performance, blended right in with the Girdwood locals during the 1986 filming.

Ken Osuna

▲ Ken Osuna

▼ Fifteen miles, North America's longest highway tunnel, and a different mindset separate GIrdwood from Whittier, which has aggressively marketed itself in recent years. The community successfully lured cruise ships to a new dock and attracted a new, upscale inn.

Ken Osuna's beat takes him to extremes.

Reporter, editor, and publisher of the twice-monthly *Turnagain Times* newspaper, Osuna covers events in Girdwood and Whittier, two neighboring but very different communities separated by a mountain and North America's longest highway tunnel.

"These two communities are very diverse, very vocal," he said. "Whittier is much more of a blue-collar town where people are busy trying to make a living and are much more in favor of development and growth.

"Girdwood is very divided, which makes it difficult to move forward. Its population is much more educated, which can be as bad as it is good. Some people have way too much time on their hands and too much money and only focus on trying to stop things."

Change has come to both communities in radically different forms. "Whittier is a town in transition now that the tunnel gives it daily access to

the rest of the highway system. A new upscale inn, new small-boat harbor, new day harbor, new cruise ship harbor.

"Girdwood's residential population has grown but its business base has shrunk."

Life as a small-town publisher poses challenges not found in other places for this transplanted Oregonian with a background in radio. Like the time a series of avalanches isolated Girdwood for a week. "I'm trying to cover the avalanche at the same time the power's out, and I'm trying to stoke the fireplace and still get my paper out on time."

Few small newspapers make a lot of money but that's okay with Osuna. "There's the beauty of this place, its mountain setting and really, really interesting people."

▲ Summer flowers and a colorful sign welcome visitors to Girdwood, a town of diverse viewpoints and deep passions. While the town's residential base has grown in recent years, its business community remains relatively stagnant.

Sewell "Stumpy" Faulkner

His ribald humor knew no bounds but underneath all the pranks and jokes was a brilliant businessman, extraordinary civic leader, and enthusiastic skier.

A Harvard graduate who drove to Alaska in 1955 with his pregnant wife and a dog in heat, Faulkner went to work selling real estate for a broker. He bought the firm in 1970 when it had annual sales of $2 million and sold it fifteen years later with sales of $200 million.

Faulkner loved life with zest, just like he loved Alaska, his family, skiing, dogs, children, and women—not necessarily in that order. He liked to hand out rolls of toilet paper [450-sheet, two-ply] and olives at Christmas time, along with hundreds of handmade holiday wreaths. "Big shots got two wreaths because they have big doors," he said.

His hunting buddies nicknamed him Stumpy because he would outwalk them and then sit on a stump until they caught up.

He helped start the Anchorage Nordic Ski Club, hosting some of the earliest races from his home in Bootleggers Cove, and was an early skier at Alyeska. He helped push Anchorage's first bid for the Winter Olympics, in 1964.

Faulkner moved into his Girdwood ski cabin in 1973. With the help of a pack dog and a twelve-inch chainsaw, he built miles of trails for hiking and cross-country skiing. In a town that rarely agrees on anything, there was widespread support to name the trail network after him, ignoring the fact he often called his neighbors Girdweirdians.

Always active in the community, Stumpy was a member of the Anchorage City Council when the 1964 earthquake hit. He also served on the Anchorage Borough Assembly and the Girdwood Board of Supervisors. He founded the Notch Club, Outfall Sewer Yacht Club, Church of New Truth, and the LAMB Club [that's LAMB as in Lost A Million Bucks]. Thousands mourned the death of Stumpy Faulkner in the year 2000.

Sewell "Stumpy" Faulkner

Over the Ridge and into the Future

The potential is apparent to anyone who sneaks a peek. Three thousand acres of the world's best ski terrain lie just around the corner from Alyeska.

Girdwood's next chapter will feature the Glacier-Winner Creek area, where a slightly higher elevation and a greater setback from Turnagain Arm solve weather problems that make Alyeska so fickle.

Chugach Powder Guides takes a few hundred skiers into the area each year. The resort encouraged Dave Hamre, its former snow safety director, to form the company to offer adventure skiing through guided helicopter and snow cat trips.

"Chugach Powder Guides cultivates new business for Alaska in high-end national and international markets," said Chris von Imhof, Alyeska's vice president and managing director.

Alyeska pioneered airplane and helicopter skiing

in North America in the 1950s, well before the mountain's first ski lift was built. Eagle and Portage Glaciers were favorite destinations, along with Max's Mountain, named for Olympic skier Max Marolt.

Per Bjorn-Roli was another of the early daredevils who raced down Max's Mountain until family responsibilities forced him to get a real job. Today he chairs a group that supports environmentally responsible development of a four-season destina-tion resort that includes a golf course. Valley golf has long been a dream of George McCoy, who organized the Girdwood Golf Association in the 1980s.

Girdwood's most famous resident is Alaska U.S. Senator Ted Stevens, the most senior Republican senator and chairman of the Senate Appropriations Committee. As von Imhof notes, "He's been a good friend of the community."

The Glacier-Winner Creek area is ideal ski country, with much of its terrain classified as beginner or intermediate. Its higher altitude base receives 55 percent more snow than Alyeska.

Per Bjorn-Roli

Taking the Next Step

He knew it was the future the first time he saw it.

"So phenomenal you could clearly see that's where we have to go."

It was the early 1960s and Per Bjorn-Roli, a Norwegian immigrant who served his U.S. military obligation helping airmen learn to ski, had his first look at the Glacier-Winner Creek area.

"A unique opportunity," says Dave Hamre, who operates a helicopter and snow cat business in the area.

Considered by resort planners to be the greatest ski opportunity in North America, Glacier-Winner Creek contains more than three thousand acres of ski terrain, including a one-hundred-acre glacier that offers a summer skiing component.

"There's only a handful of summer skiing opportunities in the world and none can compete with this jewel," says Bjorn-Roli. "It's the obvious next step in the recreational development of the Girdwood area."

Located less than a mile and a half from Alyeska, the site is simply spectacular. At 5,000 feet, the total vertical rise is greater than at any other ski area in the United States. Much of its ski terrain is classified as beginner or intermediate, making it particularly appealing to visitors. Annual snowfall is more than seven hundred inches.

In short, it's just about perfect.

Development of Glacier-Winner Creek, along with a golf course and related retail and commercial growth, would turn Girdwood into a four-season destination resort with the capacity of attracting almost as many winter visitors as summer ones.

"We have the basic ingredients," says Alyeska's Chris von Imhof. "We just need to enhance what we have and create a real village."

That's the goal of Girdwood 2020, a group of Girdwood business and property owners that Bjorn-Roli organized in 2000 to promote environmentally responsible development. Bjorn-Roli chairs Girdwood 2020, which supports development of Glacier-Winner Creek and the related infrastructure needed to turn Girdwood into a destination resort. He also advises the group of state and municipal officials who are developing a plan to offer Glacier-Winner Creek land to potential developers.

"This area has more potential and better terrain than any other resort in Europe or North America but it has stood still since 1994 when the Prince Hotel and tram opened," Bjorn-Roli said. "In fact, we've gone backwards with people suing to stop the golf course, opposing a five-year lease for helicopter skiing, fighting a transportation corridor."

Bjorn-Roli is a ruggedly handsome, can-do guy who worked hard enough to retire in comfort at age fifty-four, complete with floatplane and remote lodge. But his passion is skiing and some consider him the best skier on the mountain.

"I love this mountain. I love Girdwood and this valley. I knew when I first started skiing here that we would raise a bunch of Olympians on this mountain—and we did."

Bjorn-Roli was born to ski. "Norwegians pretty much grow up on skis. It's a form of transportation." He was good from the beginning, although ski jumping was his best event in high school. He came to the United States on a student visa and found himself drafted into the military in 1962.

"When they heard I knew how to ski, they sent me to Anchorage where I ran Hillberg Ski Area for the Air Force. That was the life. I skied all day, earned some money giving ski lessons, made even more at night as a ski mechanic tuning skis, and slept in the Hillberg aid room."

When Bjorn-Roli first showed up at Alyeska, "there was one little road over Glacier Creek and a single chair. It was a very shoestring operation but Jim Branch was an awfully nice guy who gave free skiing to all the certified instructors. I was the third or fourth certified instructor in Alaska."

Bjorn-Roli was an extreme skier who got his kicks on the outer edge. "I most enjoyed exploring the terrain outside the developed area," he said. He would put climbing skins on his skis and hike straight up the mountain to Max's Ridge, or the North Face, Winner Creek, or Raven Glacier. Or he would catch a ride with Eric Barnes, who would land his plane on top of Max's Mountain and leave off his passengers, who would then push the plane over the edge so it could glide and land back down at the airport.

In the mid-1960s, Bjorn-Roli starred in *Ski West, Part II*, a Jim Rice film. "We skied Rudi's Chute for them and then Julian Maule took us out to Portage Lake. We skied across the lake behind his Volkswagen bus, then climbed Portage Glacier and skied down between the crevasses.

"Rice wanted more excitement so he asked me to turn at the end of a crevasse and spray snow on the camera lens. I did, but I broke through the crevasse and fell about twenty feet. I would have died if the little snow bridge I landed on had failed." His fall is one of the film's highlights.

Bjorn-Roli's ski-bum days ended when he fell in love with Gayle, a fellow Norwegian, who wanted to know how he planned to take care of his family. He joined New York Life and quickly moved through the insurance company's ranks. He worked in New York City, Canada, and Oregon, and finally returned to Alaska as state manager for the company. He and Gayle raised three children, one of whom made the U.S. ski team and was an Olympic likely until injuries forced her to retire.

These days he skis three to four days a week, races in the masters program, and volunteers his time to develop Glacier-Winner Creek.

"Most developers believe you can no longer build a new ski area on federal land because you just can't permit it," Bjorn-Roli said. "That's why Glacier-Winner Creek is so exciting. All the land we need to develop the area is owned by the city and the state, thanks to three men—Larry Daniels, Dave Hamre, and former Anchorage Assemblyman Jim Barnett—who had the foresight two decades ago to select this land for transfer from the federal government."

While Bjorn-Roli focuses on the long term, Alyeska's von Imhof concentrates on the mid-term. The resort owns several hundred acres of undeveloped or underdeveloped land around the base of the mountain that it wants developed under stringent guidelines.

"We believe the best way to preserve Girdwood's unique setting and community identity is to encourage careful development that adheres to strict construction and visual standards—a true village that intermingles quality shopping opportunities with an assortment of food and drink establishments and residential units all wrapped up in a pedestrian-friendly environment," von Imhof said.

"Few resorts have enough land to truly preserve its natural integrity. We do, and we plan to do it right."

Von Imhof also sees Girdwood as a sort of base camp for visitors—a launching pad for adventure to the Kenai Peninsula, Prince William Sound, and north to Denali National Park. "Girdwood can

▲ Per Bjorn-Roli streaks down Mount Alyeska in a Masters race. Some consider Per to be the best skier on the mountain. [ERIC TEELA]

◄ Girdwood resident Per Bjorn-Roli readies for a flight aboard his Cessna 206, which he keeps docked at Lake Hood in Anchorage. Bjorn-Roli, who started skiing Alyeska in 1962, organized Girdwood 2020, a group of residents and business leaders working to develop Girdwood into a four-season destination resort.

provide all the amenities the increasingly sophisticated traveling public demands, and can be a base for tour operations offering Alaskan experiences throughout the state."

A golf course is a key part of Girdwood's future. Dreams of building a world-class golf course in the Girdwood area date back to 1965 when residents moved their town up-valley following the devastating Good Friday earthquake of 1964.

Little progress was made until the 1980s, when George McCoy and other enthusiasts organized the Girdwood Golf Association and asked the Anchorage Heritage Land Bank to investigate golf's potential. The land bank, which manages the five thousand acres of municipally owned land in the valley, contracted with Robert Trent Jones II International to identify suitable sites. The firm found two "very attractive" sites, one a short distance from the

Alyeska Prince Hotel and the second in the lower valley, straddling both sides of Glacier Creek.

A subsequent economic study concluded that an eighteen-hole course would be feasible with heavy use from both resident and visiting golfers.

The Municipality of Anchorage selected Glacier Valley Development Corp. to develop an eighteen-hole course, clubhouse, driving range, and associated residential and commercial development. Environ-mental organizations successfully challenged the lease, thus delaying the project.

In the meantime, Bjorn-Roli continues to plan for the future of Glacier-Winner Creek—including a tramway and other amenities that could unlock the exciting skiing opportunities on the site's hundred-acre glacier. "Riding the tram to the top of this glacier—where you can see into Canada—could become the biggest visitor attraction in Alaska."

The Glacier-Winner Creek area contains more than three thousand acres of potential prime ski terrain, including a hundred-acre glacier that offers a summer skiing component. Glacier-Winner Creek is just 1.4 miles from the Alyeska Prince Hotel. In this view looking east, the Glacier Creek area is at left, Winner Creek is in the middle, and Alyeska's Roundhouse is on the far right ridge.

Dave Hamre

▲ Dave Hamre

▶ Far North Ski Guides offered the first helicopter-guided backcountry treks in the 1970s. The brainchild of Dave Scott, the company took skiers into the Glacier and Goat Basin areas. The operation was the predecessor of Chugach Powder Guides.

People can die if they don't listen to Dave Hamre, a big, blue-eyed, reformed ski bum who is one of America's top avalanche experts.

Avalanche expert isn't a typical career path, but it made sense for this son of a Montana forester. "I started skiing at three," he said, "back when they had rope tows, and decided I wanted to be a ski bum for a while so took off for Alta [Utah]."

He was a ski patrolman in a high-risk avalanche area who played tunes on his mandolin at night for free beer and companionship. He served a year-long apprenticeship with the snow safety director and was promoted to safety director, a position he held for six years. Alyeska then recruited him and he spent five years as the resort's safety director.

It was a worthy challenge because the unexpected is the expected on the serious avalanche terrain around Alyeska. "There was the time that Max's face released during an employee party and the snow almost came into the day lodge."

And there was the day in March 1979 when Hamre stood at the top of Alyeska and watched one huge avalanche after another boom out into Turnagain Arm. "We were very lucky that day that the road was closed, because those avalanches came off at 150 mph and ended up three-quarters of a mile in the inlet."

Hamre now works for the Alaska Railroad, maintains an avalanche consulting business, and co-owns Chugach Powder Guides, a helicopter and snow-cat adventure ski operation. And when he has some free time, he and his wife, Patty, call together the other members of Anchor Steam, a band they formed ten years ago. "Limited performances these days, but such good friends."

Chugach Powder Guides

◄ A helicopter flies above a lone skier and the slopes of the Glacier-Winner Creek area, with its high-quality dry powder skiing. Chugach Powder Guides starts its snow-cat skiing in mid-December as snow conditions allow. Helicopter skiing begins in late January or early February and ends in mid-April. [MARK WEAVER, WARREN MILLER ENTERTAINMENT]

▼ A helicopter prepares to drop more skiers in the backcountry near Mount Alyeska. [KEN GRAHAM]

Skiers describe it in superlatives:

"Mecca for skiers and snowboarders looking for the ultimate ride."

"Snowy equivalent to what Hawaii's North Shore is to surfing."

This is Chugach Powder Guides territory—750 square miles of the western Chugach Mountain Range, a mixture of gentle bowls, giant mountain faces, massive glaciers, and sheltered tree skiing.

Dave Hamre and his partner, Mike Overcast, operate Chugach Powder Guides, which offers guided helicopter and snow-cat skiing throughout its exclusive permit area, including Glacier-Winner Creek. The company, with an international reputation for providing exceptional adventure, routinely draws clients from Europe and Asia as well as North America.

Many clients return again and again, drawn by an experience one described this way: "Part controlled fall, part bounding down a pillowy staircase of clouds, the ride is surely the closest earthbound sensation to escaping gravity."

Its safety program is one of the best in the world, thanks to avalanche expert Hamre. "We are conservative, we are older, and we have a lot of experience. What a lot of avalanche experience does for you is it makes you more and more conservative."

Hamre started Chugach Powder Guides in the late 1990s with the encouragement of the Alyeska resort, which wanted to expand winter opportunities for its guests. The business prospered, thanks in part to partner Mike Overcast, described by one reporter as "big, blond and brawny, with eyes like a Siberian husky and a calm, commanding presence."

"Mike reminds me of my younger self," Hamre said, "plus he's been on the U.S. ski team and is an experienced heli-ski guide."

Aircraft Skiing

Alyeska skiers used aircraft for ski lifts long before the first chairlift went in.

In the spring of 1958, François de Gunzburg introduced regularly scheduled helicopter skiing in Girdwood—a North American first. Ski planes flew adventurers onto area glaciers during the 1960s and the first helicopter-guided backcountry treks appeared in the 1970s.

There were some fanciful variations on the aircraft-skiing theme.

"Alyeska Air Service's second annual Glacier Polka Party will come off—weather permitting—on Sunday, June 25," reported the June 1967 *Glacier Valley Gazetta*. "Skiers will be airlifted from the Girdwood International Airport to mile-high Eagle Glacier or to Portage.

"There will be concertina music by Polka Dan, refreshments of various sorts, sunshine, good companionship and all the skiing your legs can take."

By the early 1970s, Alyeska Air Service had added a helicopter to its fixed-wing fleet.

"Alyeska Air Service, with its long history of glacier flying by ski-plane, has stationed a four-passenger helicopter at Alyeska for use this winter," according to a 1973 story in *The Anchorage Times*.

"While helicopter skiing is termed expensive, it offers an experience in skiing not otherwise attainable short of some tough climbing."

Holding tight to a rope tied to Jim Cassidy's small plane, a bunch of skiers get set for a thrilling tow across Portage Lake in April 1966. Loverne Bercee describes what happened as the plane started taxiing: "Suddenly we could feel the water building up under the thawing ice and it started getting rougher and rougher. Then someone at the front lost his footing. Down he went with everyone behind falling like dominos. We got back up on our skis and Jim coasted very slowly to the far side of Portage Lake." [CHARLES MULL]

Senator Ted Stevens

"He visits when he's here and we smoke cigars and swap stories."

Stevens is the most senior Republican senator, having served in the U.S. Senate continuously since 1968. He and Catherine made Girdwood their permanent residence in 1983.

It's not unusual for Stevens to assist Girdwood and the resort. In recent years he secured funding for a new post office and road money for paving and drainage.

◄ Senator Ted Stevens, left, with ski instructor Jim Sandberg.

▼ Barby Bowers skis along Glacier Creek. Nordic (cross-country) skiing is a popular sport in the Girdwood area, which offers miles of trail mostly maintained by volunteers. Preliminary plans call for a new, World Cup-class Nordic complex in Glacier Valley's upper reaches.

O ne of the world's most influential men calls Girdwood home.

U.S. Senator Ted Stevens and his wife, Catherine, live in a modest A-frame that they expanded a few years ago to make room for the eleven grandchildren.

"Where else would your U.S. senator neighbor call you up and ask if you could bring some tools over to help him fix a household emergency?" asks Larry Daniels, the Alyeska ski area's general manager. "Then you end up talking for an hour and a half."

"He's been a good personal friend and a good friend of the community," says Chris von Imhof, Alyeska's vice president and managing director. "We first met when I was director of tourism [for Alaska]. Ted was in the state legislature then and when I moved back to Anchorage, he offered me his log cabin until I could find a place of my own.

George McCoy

▲ Dick and Sali Day pose outside the Girdwood home they bought and remodeled in 1998-99. The Days represent a major demographic change in Glacier Valley. Longtime realtor George McCoy said residential sales shifted from second homes to primary homes in the late 1980s, and 80 percent of his sales now are to full-time residents. Many of today's buyers, like the Days, have jobs that don't require a daily commute to Anchorage. Dick is an orthodontist with a limited practice and Sali is an interior designer.

In his younger days, he was the accordion half of Two Loose Moose, a local musical favorite at the Double Musky Inn. Today he is the valley's senior real-estate agent and a positive force for change in Girdwood.

George McCoy, who holds a Ph.D. in biology, first saw Girdwood's tourism potential almost three decades ago when he sold his house in Anchorage and moved to the small community.

"This valley had resort written all over it," he said.

McCoy is one of a small group of old-timers who has worked hard to build and improve the community. "When I first arrived, we had raw sewage in the streams, the schoolhouse roof leaked, and the water wasn't potable. The drive to Anchorage was a white-knuckle experience.

"Life is much more civil now and there's a real sense of community."

Affectionately known as "the grump" by some, McCoy likes to sip scotch and talk about his favorite pastimes—hunting, golfing, and skiing. But it is his serious side that brought progress to Girdwood.

McCoy spent nine years on the Heritage Land Bank, six years on the Girdwood Board of Supervisors, served as president of Girdwood Rotary, and is a founding member of the Girdwood Golf Association.

Today he focuses on development of the Glacier-Winner Creek area and a new golf course. "That's the future," he says.

▲ George McCoy [DARYL PEDERSON]

▶ The community of Girdwood has grown rapidly in recent years and little private land is available for additional expansion. The Municipality of Anchorage owns 5,000 acres of land in Girdwood, including a large tract in the lower valley earmarked for a golf course and 1,000 acres in the Glacier-Winner Creek area suitable for resort development.

1741—Naval explorers Vitus Bering and Alexei Chirikof sight Alaska.

1778—Captain James Cook explores Cook Inlet and Turnagain Arm.

1784—Russia establishes its first major settlement in Alaska, at Kodiak.

1848—Russians discover gold along the Kenai River.

1867—Russia sells Alaska to the United States for $7.2 million.

1884—Organic Act gives Alaska its first civil government.

1896—Irish immigrant James Girdwood arrives in the Cook Inlet area.

1897-1900—Klondike gold rush in Yukon Territory.

1897—First mining claims filed on Crow Creek.

1900—James Girdwood files claims at the head of Crow Creek.

1907—Crow Creek Consolidated Mining Company [Crow Creek Mine] sold to the Nutter-Dawson Company.

1907—Post office opens in Girdwood; Emil Jones is first postmaster. James Girdwood forms LaTouche Copper Mining Company. President Teddy Roosevelt creates Chugach National Forest.

1909—Conrad Hores discovers first lode gold in the Crow Creek area, at site that becomes the Monarch Mine.

1910—Alaska Northern Railway reaches Kern Creek, four miles southeast of Girdwood.

1911—Copper production begins at Kennicott, owned by the Alaska Syndicate, which included Isaac and Daniel Guggenheim, friends of James Girdwood.

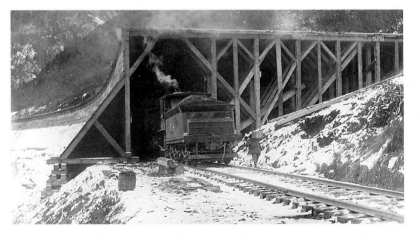

The Alaska Railroad built a long shed between Bird Point and Girdwood in 1919 to shield trains from this high-risk avalanche zone. Flumes far above the Seward Highway diverted streams around the snow shed. Only remnants remain today.

[Anchorage Museum of History and Art]

1912—The Nutter-Dawson Company incorporates as the Crow Creek Gold Mining Company [Crow Creek Mine]. Alaska gains status of U.S. territory.

1914—President Wilson authorizes construction of the Alaska Railroad; Anchorage is born as a construction campsite.

1916—Alaska Engineering Commission lays out street plan for Girdwood, with names such as Dawson Street, Gold Street, and Easy Street.

1917—Girdwood's permanent population of sixty swells to three hundred on weekends.

1922—Arne Erickson is hired to supervise operations at Crow Creek Mine.

1923—President Harding drives spike completing the Alaska Railroad, which links Alaska's population centers and brings rail service to the little town of Girdwood.

1924—Austin "Cap" Lathrop finances production of the first feature movie filmed entirely in Alaska, *The Chechahcos*, set in Girdwood.

1926—Henry Bahrenberg stakes Hottentot Mine claims.

1928—James Girdwood dies at his Clonaver home in New Jersey.

1929—Harry Staser, federal marshal, acquires Monarch Mine lode operation for $10,000, founds Crow Creek Gold Corp.

1930s—Anchorage Ski Club develops City Ski Bowl, first Anchorage ski area, with a rope tow and ski jump.

1933—Arne Erickson acquires sole ownership of Crow Creek Mine.

1939—Joe Danich buys a Girdwood roadhouse and renames it the Little Dipper.

1940s—Military opens Arctic Valley ski area, with rope tow, small lodge, and outhouse.

Mid-1940s—Joe Danich acquires Monarch Mine and operates it until the late 1940s, when mining operations cease.

1951—Seward Highway opens, linking Seward with Anchorage and passing through Girdwood. Census counts seventy-nine residents in the Girdwood area.

1955—Joe Danich builds the Girdwood Airstrip at the entrance to Glacier Valley.

1955—Early Alyeska promoter Ernie Baumann files paperwork to secure land for resort base.

1956—Bureau of Land Management sells 160 acres of Alyeska's base and lower mountain to Alyeska Ski Corp., formed by a group of eleven Girdwood families. Group punches road to mountain base and installs a 1,300-foot rope tow.

1957—French baron François de Gunzburg reorganizes Alyeska Ski Corp., with initial investment of $200,000 to build new lifts and day lodge.

Two summer tourists ride Alyeska's chairlift during a rainy day in 1968. Summer riders provided important revenue during the nonskiing season—and the resort provided rain ponchos. [*The Anchorage Times*]

Girdwood population stands at twenty-seven adults and twenty-eight children.

Charlie Willis takes over Alaska Airlines.

1959—Alaska becomes the 49th state.

Poma lift is installed at Alyeska by French lift maker Jean Pomagalski.

1960—Mile-long Chair 1 opens.

François de Gunzburg brings Winter Olympic champions Penny Pitou and Betsy Snite up for a visit to Alyeska.

Ernie Baumann dies in plane crash near Kotzebue.

Girdwood population stands at sixty-three.

1961—Alyeska hosts its first International Airlines Ski Races.

Local voters unanimously approve Girdwood's incorporation as a city; incorporation plan reports 52 permanent residents and 266 property owners; Joe Danich is elected mayor.

1962—Alyeska Ski Corp. acquires 233 acres of land from the state; first day lodge is built near the base of Chair 1.

Bob Bursiel becomes Girdwood's second mayor.

1963—Alyeska hosts National Alpine Championships and Olympic trials.

1964—Good Friday earthquake drops terrain at Girdwood by seven feet, requiring relocation of the town.

1965—Chris von Imhof becomes director of tourism for the State of Alaska.

1966—State replaces the old gravel road to Alyeska with a paved highway.

1967—Alyeska Ski Corp. signs three-year management contract with Alaska Airlines; Chris von Imhof is named general manager.

Crow Creek Mine opens to the public.

1968—Oil is discovered at Prudhoe Bay in far-northern Alaska.

1969—The thirty-two-room Nugget Inn opens at Alyeska.

Ed Gendzwill is elected mayor of Girdwood.

1970—Alaska Airlines purchases the Alyeska resort; Bruce Ficke completes forty-three condominium units at the resort.

Girdwood's population grows to 144.

Chugach State Park is created, bordering Girdwood on the west.

Bob Bursiel is again elected mayor of Girdwood.

A temporary bridge crosses Glacier Creek after the 1964 Good Friday earthquake destroyed the original bridge and severely damaged both the Seward Highway and the Alaska Railroad, leaving Girdwood isolated for a week. Alyeska Highway, which connects the resort with the Seward Highway, was reconstructed and expanded in 1965. [ANCHORAGE MUSEUM OF HISTORY AND ART]

1971—Alaska Native Claims Settlement Act passes Congress, granting title to 40 million acres of land and providing almost $1 billion in payment to Alaska Natives.

1972—Completion of 3,500-foot Chair 2 gives Alyeska skiers access to upper bowls.

1973—World Cup Giant Slalom Ski Race is held at Alyeska.
   Avalanche wipes out Alyeska's Chair 2.
   First Iditarod Trail Sled Dog Race from Anchorage to Nome.

1973—Chair 3 offers access to Alyeska's beginner slopes.

1975—Girdwood and Alyeska become part of the Municipality of Anchorage.
   First Girdwood Forest Fair.

1976—Chair 4 sets record as longest chairlift ever built in North America, with a vertical rise of 1,346 feet and a total length of 4,564 feet.
   Alaska Airlines spends more than $1 million on capital improvements, including a remodel of the Nugget Inn.

A hiker pauses near mining relics along the Iditarod Trail, which winds through Girdwood before heading over Crow Pass to Eagle River. Thousands of gold seekers made the five-hundred-mile trek from Seward to the goldfields of Interior Alaska between 1911 and 1925. This 22.5-mile segment that begins just above James Girdwood's gold property is one of Alaska's most popular trails.

Don Haglund, munching an unlit cigar, tows a rescue sled in 1983 as part of his safety work at Alyeska. Haglund has helped build every chairlift at Alyeska except for Chair 1 and has worked in avalanche control and safety since shortly after the 1964 Good Friday earthquake. An avid outdoorsman, Haglund climbed Mount McKinley in 1969 and became weathered in for ten days at 17,000 feet. Conditions were perfect on the next McKinley climb, in 1974: "thirty-two degrees above, plenty of cigars, a fifth of whiskey, and absolute calm at 20,320 feet." [JIM LAVRAKAS, *ANCHORAGE DAILY NEWS*]

1977—First oil flows through the 1,800-mile trans-Alaska oil pipeline from Prudhoe Bay to Valdez.

1978—Girdwood gets a new fire station.

1979—Twenty-year-old Chair 1 at Alyeska is replaced; night lights are installed.

1980—Seibu Alaska Inc., part of Yoshiaki Tsutsumi's Seibu group, acquires Alyeska Resort.
   Tanaka chairlift opens.
   Girdwood's resident population grows to 577.

1981—National Alpine Championships are held at Alyeska.
   Doug Keil helps form Challenge Alaska.

1982—Seibu installs $500,000 snowmaking equipment.

1983—State transfers 5,200 acres of Girdwood area land to the Municipality of Anchorage, and the Anchorage Assembly places the acreage in the municipality-owned Heritage Land Bank for management and ultimate development.
   State completes major Seward Highway upgrade.

1985—Race Training Center opens at Alyeska.
   Alaska purchases the Alaska Railroad from the federal government for $22.3 million.

1986—The feature movie *Runaway Train* is filmed in the Girdwood area; three helicopter crew members are killed in a crash during the filming.

Alaska loses bid to host 1992 Olympic Games to Albertville, France.

1987—Alyeska resort purchases eighty acres from the Municipality of Anchorage for $1.5 million

World Masters Championship is held at Alyeska.

1988—The Spirit quad-lift is installed at Alyeska.

Alaska loses bid to host 1994 Olympic Games to Lillehammer, Norway.

1989—New day lodge opens at the base of Mount Alyeska.

United States makes best medal showing ever at World Junior Alpine Championships, held at Alyeska.

1991—Municipality of Anchorage buys out mining claims in Glacier-Winner Creek area, freeing the transfer of federal land critical to resort expansion to the state and municipality.

1992—Hilary Lindh, who trained at Alyeska, wins Olympic silver in downhill.

Alyeska Tramway and Glacier Terminal open, along with the Glacier Express Restaurant.

1994—Girdwood's Tommy Moe wins Olympic gold in downhill and silver in super giant slalom.

The 307-room Alyeska Prince Hotel opens.

1995—Challenge Alaska opens recreational sports center in Girdwood.

1998—New highway from Bird Point to Girdwood opens, eliminating major avalanche danger.

Alyeska hosts Celebrity Sports Invitational.

Ken Osuna publishes first issue of *Turnagain Times*.

1999—Rosey Fletcher of Girdwood takes a silver medal at the snowboarding World Championships.

2000—Skier Per Bjorn-Roli organizes the group Girdwood 2020 to work on plans for ski and resort development in the Glacier-Winner Creek area.

2001—Alpine skiing competition for the Special Olympics Alaska Winter Games is held at Alyeska.

Rosey Fletcher again wins a silver medal at the snowboarding World Championships.

2002—*Skiing* magazine ranks Alyeska number 1 in North America for snow conditions and number 6 for "steeps."

2003—Alyeska hosts 19th World Mountain Running Trophy Race, the first time this international championship has been held in North America.

A skier pauses above the quad lift on a sunny spring day. Spring brings long days and mild temperatures to Alyeska with a March average of thirty-two degrees Fahrenheit. The ski season typically stretches from mid-November to mid-April, with weekend skiing through Memorial Day as conditions permit.

◄ The 307-room Alyeska Prince Hotel opened in 1994 on property hand-picked by owner Yoshiaki Tsutsumi. Rooms feature heated towel racks, bathrobes and slippers, and northern lights wake-up calls. The fitness center contains a pool, sauna, 16-person mountain view spa, and a work-out room. The hotel has two full-service restaurants on the premises, along with a sushi bar, piano lounge and coffee kiosk.

About the Author

Lana Johnson

Lana Johnson, a former member of the University of Wyoming ski team, moved to Alaska in 1971, where she worked for *The Anchorage Times* as a reporter, editor, and managing editor. She moved into public relations, where she developed a keen interest in public policy issues.

She became involved in Girdwood issues while a member of the Anchorage Parks and Recreation Commission, and later represented the Municipality in the formation of the Girdwood master plan.

She and husband Don moved to Girdwood full time in 2003.

About the Photographer

Randy Brandon [BARBY BOWERS]

Randy Brandon arrived at Girdwood in the summer of 1972 with a backpack and one hundred dollars. He held down a variety of ski area jobs before working his way into photography.

Like many professional photographers, he started shooting photos for fun. Experience led to an increasing number of paid assignments and in 1980 he became a full-time professional photographer. He is owner of Third Eye Photography in Girdwood.

While Girdwood and Mount Alyeska remain favorite subjects, Brandon has shot throughout Alaska and in South America, Japan, Mexico, China, Canada, Europe, Israel, Australia, and New Zealand. On an assignment to document a circumpolar expedition, he traveled to Russia, Finland, Sweden, Norway, Iceland, Greenland, Canada, and back to Alaska in a period of seven days.

His photographs have appeared in major magazines and tourism publications, including *National Geographic* and *Alaska* magazines.

▶ Winter's alpenglow turns Turnagain Arm into a fairyland. The best view of any ski area in North America, said *Conde Nast Traveler* magazine. Alyeska's base is a mere 250 feet above sea level, but its 2,500 vertical feet of skiable terrain makes it one of the top three "tough" mountains in North America.

▼ Girdwood's scenic Virgin Creek tumbles over a ledge and into a gorge. The creek originates in a small side valley at the lower eastern side of Glacier Valley and flows directly into Turnagain Arm. The creek was named in the late 1890s after a gold miner.